MY JOURNEY

MY JOURNEY

Or How A Mischievous Preacher's Son Came To
Preach The Glorious Gospel On Three Continents

BY DR. JAMES C. DODD

TATE PUBLISHING & *Enterprises*

Published by Tate Publishing & Enterprises, LLC
127 E. Trade Center Terrace | Mustang, Oklahoma 73064 USA
1.888.361.9473 | www.tatepublishing.com

Tate Publishing is committed to excellence in the publishing industry. The company reflects the philosophy established by the founders, based on Psalms 68:11,
"The Lord gave the word and great was the company of those who published it."

Published in the United States of America

ISBN: 978-1-60247-562-5
1. Christian: Autobiography   2. Church Life

07.09.07

From the Author ...

When I agreed to write "my story" it was with some qualms. I knew it necessitated my telling at least some of my misadventures, the unpleasant as well as the joyful. So, here it is from its very beginning.

When I recall my boyhood as a preacher's kid, the adventures come tumbling out of my memory. I cannot fault my parents for they were wonderful, loving and dedicated. They administered discipline as needed! No doubt some said, "What a mischievous kid, but after all he's a preacher's kid!" These daring acts followed into my teen years. Some of my adventures were exciting, but some were stupid, even putting my life in danger. Some I regret, but they are recounted here to magnify the grace of God and His ability to take anyone who will submit to His will and use them to accomplish His will.

You will see a lot of family photos. I wanted to emphasize God's desire for us to have happy, Christian families. We have always been a happy family! Precious memories!

This story takes us from childhood through a journey that includes a wonderful marriage to my sweetheart of seventy years, shared experiences of pastoring, missions work in the raw, preaching in the jungles of Africa, ministering in some of the greatest churches on three continents, superintendent of the great Oklahoma District of the Assemblies of God, serving in various capacities of leadership in our national organization, including the General Presbytery Board. I am a member of that illustrious group for my lifetime.

God is a good God! He has been so good to me to allow me these wonderful blessings. So, enjoy *My Journey* with me!

Acknowledgements

I express my deepest gratitude to these who have helped in a very significant way as I wrote my memories of *My Journey.*

1. To my daughters, Jimmie and Barbara, who for years have urged me to write this book, "So that our future family generations will have a testimony of the power of God, of miracles, of the guidance of the Holy Spirit in the life of their grandfather!"

2. To Mary Bush St. Louis, who is a genius of computer imaging, producing these wonderful full color photos, in their proper size. They enhance the presentation tremendously.

3. To Bob Eskridge, who took the beautiful photos of Jerusalem and Petra while accompanying us on a thrilling Holy Land trip.

4. To one of Tulsa's great doctors, Mary Anne Lewis, Ed. D. Consulting Psychologist. She has helped me so much since my sweetheart's home going. Listening to my stories she insisted, "You *must* write a book! All your life, from infancy, through adolescence, teen years, courtship and marriage, ministry to the church, business ventures, have all exhibited a 'spirit of daring' that is so unusual it will undoubtedly inspire others to excellence, to never settle for mediocrity."

5. To Bob Stinchcomb—an excellent photographer—who helped tremendously in various parts of this endeavor. Cover photo by Bob Stinchcomb.

Foreword

Oklahoma District
Superintendent
Rev. H. Franklin Cargill
and wife Linda

The Psalmist David declared—"The steps of a good man are ordered by the Lord: and he delighteth in his way."

Every person, without exception, leaves behind footprints in the sands of time.

It matters not the age, the background, nor even the epitaph inscribed in stone. The "marks" of all who live—remain.

Two special individuals walked as pilgrims through this world, and thousands of those who follow have never been the same. The lives of James and Francine Dodd stand as a tribute to the grace and the power of an awesome God.

Their personal story is documented in the pages to follow. It is the account of two special people who walked hand-in-hand in pursuit of their dreams. They sought not fame or recognition but were consumed with a passion birthed by an unquenchable fire. They have provided a path to follow and demonstrated excellence worthy of imitation.

The personal account of James C. Dodd, as told in his own words, will move one to tears as well as to action. His life is a tribute to his pursuit of a personal relationship with Jesus Christ.

Reverend James C. Dodd might well be classified as one of the greatest orators of the twentieth century. He fills the pulpit with grace and dignity. His speech is laced with descriptive terms and picturesque vocabulary. His voice is unmistakable and clearly recognizable whether in a congregation of people, when producing a radio program, or at the receipt of a personal phone call.

Francine Dodd personified the descriptive words of Solomon as he defined a virtuous woman in the thirty-first chapter of Proverbs. Francine received her promised reward in heaven when she breathed her last breath of terrestrial air on November 5, 2005.

She was devoted to her husband, her family, and never shirked at the responsibilities committed to her trust. She was filled with poise and beauty not only in her appearance but in her speech and her personal relationships. It is almost impossible to speak of one of them without naming the other.

Together, the Dodds have made a lasting impression on the Fellowship of the Assemblies of God. Side by side they blazed a trail across Oklahoma and the surrounding states as they responded to the call of God upon their lives for full-time ministry. Perhaps they are best remembered for their thirty-six years of pastoral ministry in Broken Arrow as they led a small band of people in establishing the great church that it has become today.

In addition to pastoral duties, Reverend Dodd served the Oklahoma District Council of the Assemblies of God as Assistant District Superintendent for twenty-seven years. In 1980, he assumed the role of District Superintendent, where he labored faithfully for the next three years.

Since 1953, Brother Dodd has represented the Assemblies of God as a General Presbyter by serving on the highest policy-making body of the church. In 1985, he was elected to that position as an honorary member, a position which he will continue to hold as long as his days on earth remain.

Thousands of people are in heaven today as a result of his ministry. Untold numbers of young men and young women have responded to the call of God by entering the ministry under his influence. His commission to take the Gospel to the ends of the earth has resulted in lives transformed not only throughout America but around the world.

The reader must hear his heart, feel his passion, and respond to the challenge as the writer unveils his life and reveals his soul. May the words of this book inspire and motivate another generation to pursue their God-given dreams in the same manner as the author.

Footprints...Yes, without question! The "steps" of James and Francine Dodd are clearly visible.

I am proud to say that James C. Dodd is my hero!

I am humbled as I trace his steps but grateful for the mentorship that Brother and Sister Dodd have provided for Linda and me.

-Rev. H. Franklin Cargill
Oklahoma District Superintendent,
Assemblies of God

My Journey

I was born March 11, 1918, in Fayetteville, Arkansas. My parents were Reverend and Mrs. Berl Dodd, and they instilled in me, at a very early age, a work ethic that has contributed much to whatever success I have achieved.

We are all products of our forbears and associates. We are influenced by the lives that have been lived before us. So, I must tell you a little about the ones who went before me and also of the ones who were my close contemporaries.

I had one brother and two sisters.

Berniece was the first born. I remember her as a pretty young lady, with luxurious hair that cascaded to her waist. She was demure and a little bashful. Of course, she wanted to blend in with her peers. But, it wasn't an easy thing, considering the protective father we had. I well remember one wintry day, Dad coming to her class after her because she had left off one of her petticoats! She was past embarrassment ... she was mortified.

Because of her being the oldest one, she was given the task of helping take care of me when I came along five years later. She walked many a mile carrying me on her hip.

One day we were walking the railroad track to cut across to our destination when I got my foot wedged under a rail. And, a train was coming to meet us! It was a scary time indeed. But, Berniece knelt between the rails and worked my foot out of my shoe, and I was safe.

In retrospect, I am quite sure that I made her life miserable when her boyfriends came calling. I know she's in heaven, and I'll probably have to apologize before they'll let me in.

She was first ... I came along next. It seemed that my little life would start off quite unpleasant. In those days, every mother nursed her baby.

There was no such thing as formula in baby bottles. My mother had very little milk, and I was always hungry.

One day a lady who lived quite a ways away came to see us. I was fretting and crying. She asked mother the reason for my unhappiness. Mother explained the situation. Before anyone could stop her, she picked me up, unloosed one of her big breasts and put the nipple in my mouth!

Mother was furious … she tried to rescue her baby, but I refused to let go. I had found the fountain of life!

Another five years and my brother, Doyce, came along. He was a real joy when he was small, and, as he matured, it became evident to all that he was unusually gifted. He became a wonderful musician and excelled in everything he attempted. He fell in love with a sweet young lady, Nadine Collins, and they were married. Shortly after, he was called into service and sent overseas, where he served with distinction.

After discharge, he became a representative for a school bus company and made a success at that enterprise. Then I introduced him to a business I was in, and he became a partner. He made a huge success.

It soon became apparent that his bus job was interfering with his new enterprise, so, we have a good example of his humor … it is customary for an employer to show his appreciation to an employee when he leaves by giving him a gold watch, along with words of commendation.

This boss had been very skeptical of Doyce's new venture, so, Doyce bought a gold watch, presented it to his employer and resigned!

I loved this brother of mine, and it was heartbreaking to see his health break and finally have him leave us too soon.

But, it is comforting to me to know he was right there to welcome my sweetheart as she passed through the gate!

Two years after Doyce was born, Berline was next. She was a beautiful little girl with an abundance of curls and a ready smile. She had such a sweet disposition. As a child, she was not very well, having a bout with pneumonia and other respiratory illnesses. Her couch was positioned next to her piano, and she practiced for hours, becoming an excellent pianist and later organist.

She came to visit us at Broken Arrow. She met and fell in love with a fine young man in our church, Bob Eskridge. They were eventually married and have had a great life together.

Francine and I have often said that one of the great high points of our lives was when we went with them through the Holy Land countries and on to the Austrian Alps, the place famous for the filming of *The Sound of Music*.

Berline is now confined to one of the best nursing homes in the Tulsa area. She has accepted her condition with grace and is perfectly content. What a marvelous example she is of the sweetness of the Lord in her life.

As I see her now, I think of the time we four went to Petra, "The Rose Red City of Esau." An ancient city of such magnitude it takes your breath away. A city rich in scripture and prophesied to be the refuge for the Jews during the latter half of the antichrist's reign on earth. There, they will be safe, as he seeks to destroy them.

Without doubt, Petra is one of the outstanding marvels of the whole world. Its 350 square miles are filled with unequaled architecture that has endured for many centuries. In the Bible, Petra is called Sela.

From Amman, Jordan, we traveled "The King's Highway" to the very entrance to the city. There, we mounted Arabian horses that were provided for our descent into the city. We rode into "The Sig," a mile long entrance, into "The Red Rose City."

The Sig is near the upper part of that great valley and rises so sheer that its upper parts appear to meet. There are wonderful springs, the most famous being the "Ain Mousa" spring. This is where, according to Exodus 17:7, Moses struck the rock and water flowed out! I have drunk from and been refreshed by that spring!

The Nabateans were the first inhabitants, arriving 9,000 B.C. The Bible tells us that the Orite people settled there in the rock caves. They were driven out by the Edomites, who numbered between thirty and forty thousand.

After mounting our horses, we proceeded single file down the rocky Sig. Francine, who had never been on a horse before, was in the lead. She must have kicked her mount in the side, for he took off running as if he was in a race. She held on and I could see she was having the time of her life!

Back to my childhood…

My dad operated a grocery store when I was quite small. I always was of an inquisitive nature, and I wanted to see what was under the floor. I looked in and saw a number of bottles and I wanted them. But, I was too afraid of spiders and snakes to go in after them. So, I hired another boy to get them for me. I didn't have any money so I had to compensate him some way. I hit upon an answer. I raided my mother's hen house and gave him a dozen fresh eggs. That night at dinner time I thought the jig was up. Mother said to my father, "Berl, I just don't know what happened, but my hens didn't lay an egg today!"

I drew a sigh of relief when Dad replied, "Oh, well, those things happen … they'll make up for it tomorrow."

Mother always made homemade sauerkraut and pickles. She placed them in big crocks to season. I enjoyed slipping in and grabbing a handful and putting both sauerkraut and pickles in my overall pockets. It was good to hide out and have a private feast.

One of my uncles lived next door to us, and he always had a huge garden. One fall, I looked it over and discovered an abundance of pumpkins. I coveted them. So I spent hours pulling them off the vines, lugging them inside our house and rolling them back under the bed. It turned out that my uncle and aunt had watched the whole thing from their window. A few days later, Mother discovered the pumpkins, and I had to carry them all back and apologize. And Dad got out the old well-worn razor strap.

I preached my first sermon when I was only six years of age. I had a little red banty rooster. I found him dead one morning, and I was heartbroken. So, I put him in a shoe box and picked some wildflowers to go on top. Then, I let it be known to my little friends that we were going to have a funeral. They all came. We began the "service" by singing some songs. Then various ones gave testimonials as to what the rooster meant to them. Then I read my text, "It is appointed unto man once to die!" We were all shedding tears by this time, which made it a proper send-off for my little friend.

I guess the most regrettable "fun thing" I did was to take my bean flip and hide out in the weeds behind the church's outdoor privy. A large, overfed girl made a call there. I unloosed a small pebble in her direction, and it was a perfect hit. She screamed and came out of there as terrified as if a snake had bit her. She knew that I was the culprit and most of my regret came from the meeting I had with Dad and his razor strap.

I well remember my pal and me lying on our backs, watching the birds flying so gracefully overhead. We decided we could do the same. All we needed was to build us a pair of wings. The next few days were consumed with our planning and cutting and hammering together a pair of wings. On the fateful day we climbed to the roof of the barn with our contraption. We argued as to who would go first. He won! He jumped off the barn and spread his heavy wings for flight but landed instead in a pile of manure. It probably saved him from serious injury. The list of activities was almost endless and grew daily.

We had a large extended family of aunts, uncles, and cousins. One of my favorites was my Uncle Jim. He was an old bachelor and lived alone in a cabin on the side of a mountain. He had a bunch of hounds and enjoyed sitting around a campfire and just listening to the dogs as they treed a coon. He knew the sound of each dog's howl and could identify each one as he took the lead in the chase.

Uncle Jim had a terrible failing. At least most people thought so. I didn't share their opinion. He would get drunk every few weeks and would hunt me up and put me on his shoulders. We'd go to the store, and he would load me down with candy. I looked forward to his generous episodes. He was really a kind and happy man. I loved him.

He probably saved my life. He was at our home when a neighbor's bull dog attacked me. He had me down on my back and was on my stomach trying to get his teeth into my throat. Uncle Jim kicked him off of me.

School was easy for me, and I enjoyed bringing home top grades. In fact, my teachers either loved me or wanted me out of their class, for they skipped me through the third grade and again the first half of the sixth.

In my elementary school years, I attended West Side School in

Fayetteville, Arkansas, reputed to be the toughest in town. In fact, a few of us had attained stature as capable fighters, so we took turns challenging any new boy who came to our school.

I well remember when a tall boy, who wore glasses, joined my class. We thought he was soft because of the glasses. I was designated to try him out. We all thought he would be an easy one. So, as the group reached the first intersection after school, I stopped them and said to "Speck", "Okay, we're going to see who's the best!"

Speck answered, "I don't want to fight you; I don't have anything against you."

"That don't matter; we have to fight!"

So we squared off. Speck hit me one time on the point of my chin, and I went down. For the first time in my life I saw stars and heard the canaries sing. That was the end of that!

We dispersed and went home for lunch. As I was getting ready to go back to school, I heard someone in the front yard, whistling for me. I went to the door and there was Speck. He held a big brains and egg sandwich out to me as a peace offering. We were fast friends after that.

Big John Evans thought that he was the toughest boy in school, and he laughed at my misfortune. So he challenged Speck the next day. Same place … same time … same result. Speck was one of us then.

Mrs. Black was my teacher, and she was a good one. I loved her and respected her but, of course, would never have let her know it. She knew that I had no money, so she hired me to stay after school and cut out a big patch of briers on the backside of the school ground. She paid me twenty-five cents an hour, which was an unheard of wage for a boy as men were working for a dollar a day.

I was always looking for a way to make a few cents. I answered ads and sold every product I could get sent to me on consignment. I sold ladies' perfume in vials for ten cents. Rosebud and cloverine salve for twenty-five cents. I sold the *Grit* magazine.

But the one thing I really wanted was to be a paper boy. My folks did not think that was a good idea. So, one day I got my chance. It was in the dead of winter and was very cold. I went to town to get my shoes half-soled. I had the money in my pocket to pay for it. I took my shoes off and left them with the cobbler for repair and made my way to the newspaper office. I spent all on that day's paper and stood on a corner to sell my papers. I guess the sight of that little boy, bare-footed, gave me an edge. I quickly sold out, went back and retrieved my shoes, and had the extra profit from my papers. I guess my willingness to take chances, which followed me all my life, was even then evident.

My dad was my hero. He bought me a fly rod, and I was with him on all his fishing trips. We most usually fished the west fork of the White River between Fayetteville and the town of West Fork. He fished the deeper holes and left the more shallow ones for me. I still have that first fly rod, and it is not for sale. About half way between the two cities, there is a stretch of water called "Cotton Mouth Hole." It was a beautiful fishing hole, but nobody scarcely dared to wade it and fly fish it because of the snakes. Dad always fished it and always caught fish there. As a little bare-footed boy, I ran along the bank, and as he caught a fish, he would throw it to me. My love for fishing started here and grew.

I enjoyed being a fisherman! It was a good release for me. You actually forget all your problems when fishing. The fish you see with me and my brother-in-law in the photo section weighed eleven pounds, and we didn't waste any time getting it on the table. It was caught from Lum's big pond.

Nearly every July, my friends, Dr. Bob Goggin and Rev. Russel Herndon, and I made our annual pilgrimage to Padre Island. The king fish were running! We caught those big fighting beauties until we were exhausted. They were dressed and brought home for the skillet. You see in the photos that we also caught some hammerhead sharks. Nothing better than shark steaks. Francine also enjoyed fishing but she couldn't take the hours of preparation and the hard part of a real fishing trip, so, I would take her to northwest Arkansas to a lake stocked with trout. It kept me busy baiting her hook, along with helping the girls. The cost was $1.00 per pound for your catch. My problem was in getting them to stop! "Just let me catch one more!" But nothing was wasted. We stocked our freezer with them.

When I was about thirteen years of age, I had a life-changing experience. My father had accepted the pastorate of the Seminole church, and was holding an old-fashioned tent revival. The family had not as yet moved there. But, I went to spend the weekend with him. Naturally, I went to the revival. When I walked under the tent, the first thing that caught my eye was a group of young people across the tent. There were quite a number of them, but a beautiful little, feisty girl was the center of my attention and the leader. I was smitten, and she was the only one of the group as far as I was concerned. But I was disturbed also because I discovered that she was sitting by a young lad. But that was temporary for after the next night, she was sitting by me and holding my hand! I loved her from that first view and there was never another girl who had my serious attention.

A couple of years went by and our lives became more intertwined. I played the trombone at school and also in the church orchestra. So, Francine had her mother buy her a trombone and took lessons. Soon, she was sitting next to me with her trombone. She told one of our daughters shortly before her death, "I wanted to be with James and I certainly wasn't going to take a chance of one of the other girls getting him!"

My high school days were filled with a quest for adventure. After a football game, my friend and I were following a busload of young people from our competing school. The back door of the bus was open and a bevy of girls was waving and shouting at us. My friend maneuvered the car up close to the back of the bus. I climbed over the hood and jumped inside the open door. I could have paid with my life for that stupid trick, but we thought we were really having fun. Anyway, the girls were real friendly.

Another time, I took my father's car to school and then took some friends to the out of town football game. Coming home late, we were having fun. One friend started to come from the back seat to the front. As he was suspended in the attempt, I suddenly put on the brake and his head went through the windshield. Fortunately, his cowboy hat saved him from being cut severely. But, I knew I was in real trouble with Dad. So, I found a large rock, stood in front of the car and threw it through the hole. I really felt guilty the next morning when Dad came in saying, "Some ornery guy has thrown a rock through my car windshield. I only wish I could get my hands on him!" I felt badly but I kept quiet. I didn't tell Dad the truth until after I was married and even then, I knew he was tempted to get out the old razor strap.

Fortunately, Francine didn't know of these escapades until much later. I had a lot of repenting to do along the way.

Another year passed. I was spending most of my Sundays hanging out with Lum, her brother. One excuse was as good as another. Besides, Mom Bush's meatloaf and cherry pie with whipped cream was an added incentive.

During this time, I was saving my money. Most of it came from going without lunch and putting back my dimes. I saw a set of engagement and wedding rings in the jewelry window, priced at $15.95. Francine was so proud and happy when I presented those rings to her. They were real treasures back in that day when money was so scarce. So, we were engaged!

I'm not so sure she would have been so willing to take a chance on me if she knew the full story of my misadventures. Some of them were funny and some were so daring they were stupid. My childhood, growing up as the proverbial "preacher's kid" was so filled with the unusual that when I took her to Fayetteville after we were married, she was shocked again and again as the locals dutifully filled her in on my record!

But, through it all, our friendship continued, and we both decided that we wanted to live together for the rest of our lives. So, I went for the marriage license and much to my chagrin, they told me I "couldn't cut the mustard." I refused to lie about my age so it seemed that was it for the present time. But, Francine's brother came to our rescue. He took it upon himself to apply for me. I know he lied about my age (I was seventeen), but I never did ask him about it. I had the license in my hand...

We were in another tent revival at our church. Francine and I both played our trombones in the church orchestra that Sunday morning. Then, when the evangelist got up to preach, we slipped out the back of the tent. Lum had a car waiting for us, and we went immediately to my friend, the Justice of the Peace. I had promised him that I would have him marry us. My father, the pastor, was so taken aback that he could hardly speak. He loved Francine and had no objection to our union, but having a J.P. marry us was unthinkable! But, everyone was soon forgiving.

We went to church that night and were a part of the music ministry. Then, to my surprise and disgust, two strong armed, young men took hold of my arms and forced me into a car. They took me to a house out in the oilfields and planned on keeping me there all night, with Francine at my parent's home in town. It was fun to them, but I was seething inside. The party got going pretty strong. I slipped out a window, and they didn't miss me before I found one of the cars with the key in the ignition. I soon was reunited with my sweetheart and their party went flat.

Remember, these were the depression years and renting a house was out of the question. My parents gave us one bedroom for our first house-keeping unit. Francine brought her little suitcase of all her belongings, and we were happy and considered ourselves blessed.

But, I knew I would find a job and support us. They were hard to find, but I persevered. The going rate at most jobs was one dollar a day. One of my first positions was with the leading grocery store in town. The grocery man bought flour by the carload. His volume of business could not support such a large shipment, so his flour was soon filled with worms. Instead of taking a loss, the wily old gentleman had a large sifter set up in the back room, and I spent many hours sifting out the worms and re-bagging the flour.

My next job was on a rock crusher. My job was to wield a sledge hammer and beat the large rocks into smaller pieces that would carry on the conveyer belt. For ten hours daily I was paid one dollar. I came home so dirty and so weary that my mother and Francine both declared I could not continue.

I decided I could never reach my potential by working in such miserable conditions at such a wage.

I saw an ad in the paper from the White River Fish Company in Arkansas. When I called them, they offered to send me a fifty-five gallon drum of assorted kinds of fish. It arrived on Thursday, and I was in business. I borrowed Dad's old Dodge, took the back seat out, got pans out and sorted out my fish. Then I went through the oilfield camps and sold almost everything the first day. I made more that one day than I could make in two weeks working for somebody else. Thus was born the idea that I would henceforth work for no man but would create my own income.

My grandfather on my father's side, "Uncle" Bob Dodd as he was affectionately called by most everyone throughout the Ozarks, was an old circuit rider Methodist preacher. He kept his appointments by horse back or buggy, regardless of the weather. He was of English and Cherokee extraction.

Granddad had a brother who was also a minister. He heard of the revival at Azusa Street in Los Angeles, California, and took a train cross-country to see this spiritual phenomenon for himself. After personally receiving a wonderful baptism of the Holy Spirit, he wired my grandfather, "Bob, come on out here. This is the real manifestation of God!" The rest is history. Granddad went, received his personal baptism, with the evidence of speaking in other languages as the Spirit gave the utterance. When he came home, he enthusiastically proclaimed this new revelation. The Methodist church was not at that time ready to embrace this doctrine, so Granddad became an independent Pentecostal preacher. He died, the year I was born, as a result of fording a swollen stream on his horse, in the dead of winter. He contracted pneumonia and went on to his reward.

Grandmother Dodd came to live with us, and she became my best buddy. She was a kindly, gentle soul. As she was unable to be out and about, I stayed with her and took care of her needs while the rest of the family was away. I loved the stories she told me of those pioneer days.

I had great pioneer stock on my mother's side. Grandpa Bogan was a small, wiry man who prided himself on being self-sufficient. From French ancestry, he had a small farm and raised everything his family needed. He grew his own corn to feed his pigs and cattle, and nothing went to waste. His barns were full, and his cellar was crammed with home-canned fruits, vegetables and meats.

My Grandmother Bogan was a large, capable woman. She knew what it was to work along with Granddad, preserving and canning everything her family needed to sustain them in good health.

One of my fondest memories was of visiting them on occasion after I had married Francine and Jimmie Lee was born. About four o'clock in the morning, Grandad would knock on our bedroom door and say, "James, get up. Grandma has breakfast ready!" And what a breakfast... big sausage balls, biscuits as big as your fists, gravy and other assorted delicacies, such as homemade jams and jellies!

My father... a whole book could be written about him. He was a preacher for over sixty years, but he also was a grocery man and a building contractor. Before the Great Depression suddenly hit in 1929, he was one of the leading businessmen in Fayetteville, Arkansas. He had several houses under construction in "Dodd Addition" when the Great Depression struck. Overnight, there was no money. He rented out the homes that were ready for occupancy at ten dollars per month. He would send me to collect the rent, and I would return with nothing. We had to move out of our new brick home. To me, the greatest loss was when we had to give up the 240 acre farm he had purchased in Prairie Grove. Two of my uncles farmed it for him on shares, and I spent many happy hours swimming in the creek or riding my horse over the pastures or through the woods. Francine and I drove down there one day for the express purpose of trying to buy that farm back. But, to my disappointment, it was being cut up into small portions for individual homes.

But, Dad was foremost of all, a preacher. How he loved to preach. When I was just a small lad, I well remember going with him back into the hills for revivals. He had a forty by sixty foot tent. "We" would erect it on a hillside and get planks for seating. People would come out of those hills and Dad would preach. He did not need a microphone, his booming voice carried through those hills and valleys, and people came to see who this man was. Dad was absolutely fearless. Young toughs would cut down his tent, ignite dynamite outside as services were in progress. It didn't faze him. Later, as pastor at Seminole, he called the police many times to close a dope house or to cart away some of the dozens of whores who insisted on doing their business close to his beloved church.

My father always had a burden for missions. As a lad, I remember him and Mother entertaining missionaries from many parts of the world. In addition to giving beyond his means, he started a Bible ministry selling Bibles and contributing all the profits to missions. He continued this as long as his health would allow. Francine and I felt that we should continue supplying this after he had moved to heaven. For example, I quote from a newsletter from missionary Quentin McGhees: "Once again, Rev. and Mrs. James Dodd have given money to provide Bibles for 100 Bible school graduates in East Africa. This is in memory of their parents. What a wonderful gift to Christ!"

"Whatever you did for one of the least of these brothers of Mine, you did for Me!" (Matthew 25:40). Somehow I believe they know and are pleased.

Dad not only had a vision for missions, but he was known to have pioneered and built more churches throughout the Ozarks than any other man. His ministry was accompanied by many miracles from God. For instance, he was ministering at Grace Chapel, a church he built some miles east of Springdale, Arkansas. The country was being destroyed by a long-lasting drought. On Sunday morning, Dad announced to the congregation, "Bring your umbrellas to church tonight…it's going to rain!" The whole countryside learned of this pronouncement before night. When we came to church, it was packed with skeptics. As service began, there was not a cloud in the sky. It was the same as my father got up to preach.

Just before he reached the end of his message, there came a loud clap of thunder, lightning rent the heavens, and the rain began to pour! The drought was broken! People shed their skepticism and filled the altars with shouts of praise and thanksgiving.

My Grandfather Dodd, my father, and myself, together preached a total of more than 180 years. Oh how I wish I could do it all over again!

My mother, Ella Dodd, was just about the sweetest lady I ever knew. She saved me from many an encounter with Dad and his razor strap. During this depression, food was scarce, hobos were riding the rails, and beggars were at our door often. My mother never turned anyone away. She always gave of what she had. I have seen times when Dad would be away, preaching somewhere in the mountains, Mother would have to wait until the hens laid enough eggs for her to prepare dinner for her four children. But, she could always improvise, and we never went hungry. It was a special treat, when we had an extra dime. I would walk up the railroad track to the milk factory, where Uncle Edward worked, and bring back a gallon of milk. Mother's gentle ways as well as my father's strength made me what I am.

Francine and I went to Fayetteville, Arkansas, where I was in charge of building a store building and two residences. We lived with Vernon, my brother-in-law. My sister, Berniece, was in Seminole at that time.

Francine took on her new responsibilities cheerfully. She had never cooked on a wood-burning stove before but she learned fast. She cooked three meals a day for me, Vernon, and two men I had hired out of the hills to set logs for the store building. She always had a good meal on the table. Remember, money was scarce, but I took three dollars and bought her a fancy pair of house shoes. She was so happy as she walked up the sidewalk to my place of work. She wanted people to see her new house shoes!

I heard of a grocery store for sale in Seminole, Oklahoma, where Dad pastored, and decided I'd try to buy it. I got a "Big Chief" tablet and wrote down all the reasons I felt I would be a good risk for a loan. Then, I made an appointment with the president of our bank. I went into his office, spread out my tablet and proceeded to present my case for the loan. I'll never forget the reaction from the gentleman. He first asked, "Tell me about your personal assets that you can bring to this enterprise."

I answered, "The only asset I have is myself. I am knowledgeable about the business, and I will work day and night to make it a success." Then I got the news I didn't want to hear.

He looked at me over his horn-rimmed glasses and said very succinctly, "Young man, this is an un-bankable situation. You are only eighteen years of age and have no assets. So, I bid you good day!" I left his office disappointed but determined to find a way. And I did! I got my loan.

Francine and I moved into the two room apartment in the back of the store and were so happy as we set to work. We established a rapport

JAMES C. DODD

with the present customers and kept their goodwill and business. Then, we went after others. We put every dime we made back into increasing our stock until we had anything anyone would expect from a grocery. My wholesale meat suppliers taught me how to butcher, to display my meat to the best advantage, and Francine sat with me night after night as I prepared my meat case for the next day. It actually became a drawing card for new customers. My nearest competitors used what was commonly called "dynamite" to preserve their meat and keep it from spoiling. The Health Department emptied all their meat into the sawdust one day and that gave my business a big boost as people knew that they could trust me to never do such a thing.

We prospered. I bought a T-Model Ford pickup and began a delivery service. We also bought our first home, a pretty little cottage just across the street from the store. It cost us the big sum of $800.

While in the grocery business, I suffered from tonsillitis so much that I decided to get it over with. So, I made an appointment with Dr. Lyons, drove to his office, sat in a chair and had my tonsils removed without any anesthetic. I thought I could take any type of pain, but this was really a stretch. The doctor charged $25 and took it out in groceries. A little later Francine became pregnant with Jimmie. The same doctor ... the same charge ... the same manner of payment.

During this time Jimmie Lee was born. When she was just a toddler, she almost took over the store. It was her playhouse! Everybody, including all the people who serviced us with supplies, had to stop and visit with her. She had a little dog, Brownie, that helped her get into a lot of mischief. For example, they grabbed a big wiener from the meat case. The problem was that they were all linked together, and they both went scampering outside dragging my whole supply of wieners.

Another time, Francine was taking care of the store while I made a delivery. A gentleman came in and went toward the candy case smiling. Francine asked, "May I help you?"

And he replied, "Yes, I think I'll have some of those chocolates!" When Francine proceeded to comply with his request, she saw Jimmie lying across a thirty-pound box of chocolates, her mouth and face smeared with those she had eaten, asleep!

She loved to go with me when I made deliveries. That was before seatbelts, so she stood behind my right shoulder. One day I went around a corner pretty fast, the right-hand door came open, and she was headed out the door. I caught her by an ankle and pulled her back in.

I wasn't an ordinary storekeeper with conservative ways ... I enjoyed giving happy surprises to our customers.

One late afternoon, a man drove up to my store with a big truckload of watermelons. He wanted to sell them all and just go home. He offered me a real deal ... ten cents each if I'd take the whole load. I took it and sold the whole bunch in a couple days at twenty-five cents each.

Another time a weary trucker came to my store with a load of potatoes. They were in 100 pound sacks. I bought the entire load for fifty cents a sack and sold them out quickly for $1 each. People came from everywhere for these bargains.

I had only one strikeout. I bought a gross of straw hats. I invoiced some of them out to the people who bought my store four years later!

So, each eventful day turned into weeks, and weeks into months. Soon we had been in the grocery business for over four years. Happy years, and it seemed we were destined to become a real success.

But it seemed God had other plans for us. All this time, I had been serving as youth director at the church. I wrestled with the conviction that there was a divine calling on our lives that preempted our love for the business world. Gradually, the conviction came to me that I was supposed to be a preacher of the glorious Gospel of our Lord, Jesus Christ!

When I confided this calling to Francine, she was devastated! Her life was just what she wanted it to be. She loved the business. Our customers were her friends. The income we had supplied our family with a very comfortable living. A call to go preach was filled with uncertainties. Where would we live ... what income could we expect ... how would my ministry be received? So, she came up with the perfect solution. "You go preach ... conduct your revival meetings ... I will stay here and operate this store. You know I can, I have experienced help to assist me. I can underwrite your ministry so that you'll never have to receive an offering." But it wasn't long until she recognized the folly of such reasoning. We had to live our lives in agreement. She decided that, whatever course our future held, she was completely behind my calling and wanted to be an integral part of it. She never looked back but enthusiastically became my full partner in ministry.

So, we sold our grocery business and also our little home. We purchased a new, deluxe Chevrolet for $850 and were prepared to launch into our evangelistic ministry.

But, our future took another turn. The board of Glad Tidings Assembly of God Church in Shawnee invited us to be the pastors of that congregation. It turned out to be a real challenge.

We weren't there but a few months when I contracted typhoid fever. At that point in time there was no magic cure for this disease. It was week after week of debilitating fever that ravished my body, bringing my weight from 225 pounds to 125 pounds when I was finally released. This was a trying time for Francine. She was the only one, outside of the medical staff, allowed in my room. She faithfully stayed with me, day and night. I could not have made it without her.

The doctors gave us no hope of my leaving the hospital alive. But God! Francine said she was looking out the window late one night when she saw a group of cars pull up in the parking lot. One young lady, who was also a nurse at the hospital, came in and asked the nurse in charge about my condition. She replied, "You know it's strange but it seems he passed the crisis point tonight and if nothing happens otherwise, he may make it!"

Our nurse friend from the church replied, "He will make it. Our entire group at the church has been praying all night, and we believe that God has answered our prayers!" A few weeks of recuperation and I was once more in the pulpit. What a miracle!

Other miracles followed. We were in a desperate race to raise money to pay off the mortgage on the church before it was due. The people responded, giving their money, their rings, their watches. Francine organized the ladies to bake pies to sell. They delivered those beautiful and nutritious pies all over town, selling them for thirty-five cents.

When it became evident that our people had given all they could possibly give as cash, I made an appeal for personal gifts of jewelry, watches, etc. My wife's brother, Lum, who had just returned from service, was the first one who walked down the aisle to put a cherished ring on the altar. That started an avalanche of gifts that helped put us over the top. His wife, Ethel, always was as generous as he was. Through the years of their marriage, she stood behind him in every decision he made.

It was the last day before the money was due. We had raised every cent we possibly could and were still $500 short. My phone rang, and a lady, whom I had never met, had never been in our church said, "Pastor Dodd, would you please come by my home?" I followed her directions to her palatial home. When I rang the doorbell, she came to the door and handed me an envelope. That was all ... no explanation. When I returned to my study and opened the envelope, there was no writing, nothing except a check for $500! A miracle!

Right after going into the ministry, we went to Fayetteville. We sadly learned of a tragic event that had the whole community upset and many crying out for immediate justice.

As a boy, we lived near the fairgrounds. Just beyond our garden, Sam Sweeney lived for many years. He had a lovely home, was well-respected and was boss over the large hardwood mill that supplied employment for most of the men in the community.

There was a large hydrant at the mill where many people came for their water. Many were negligent and would leave quite a mess and this made Sam unhappy.

A small lad, belonging to the Stout family, came for water and was letting it run all over everything. Sam thought, *This is a time to scare that kid and stop this.* He had a small penknife in his hand. As he struck out with his hand, somehow the knife penetrated the head just behind the ear and he killed he child.

The community was furious. Sam was out on bail but was afraid to show himself outside his home. There was talk of a lynching. Sam armed himself for defense.

I grieved for the Stouts for they were good friends but also wanted the opportunity to talk with Sam, my friend from my childhood. Everyone spurned and hated him.

I purposed to get to see him and his wife and tell them that Jesus still loved them in spite of circumstances, would forgive him if he called on him. I was strongly advised to stay away ... that Sam was heavily armed and would take no chances with any visitors. But, I was determined to go; I felt it was my duty.

So, that night I made my way alone to his front gate. There was no light in the house and the night was pitch black. I stood at the gate and cried out, "Sam, this is James Dodd. Remember I lived for years as your neighbor? I want to see you!" There was no answer and the house remained dark. Two more times I called out before I got any response. Then I heard Sam say, "James, if that is really you, come closer if there is no one with you." He opened the door and laid down his gun and let me in. I talked with them for quite a while, emphasizing the love of God and His willingness to forgive any sin. With tears and sincere prayer we talked to God in Sam's behalf. Sam went to prison for a long, long time. I can only pray that our concern for his soul stayed with him and brought relief.

Meanwhile, our Oklahoma District Council convened at the convention center in Seminole, and I was in charge of all the services. At prayer time, I announced that we would be praying for healing after the regular time of united prayer and that those who wished to be prayed for individually to please come on the platform. I watched as two men carried a young soldier up the steps and stood him before me. I later learned that this man was Paul Sturgeon and that he had been severely injured by falling off a cliff when engaged in maneuvers. The diagnosis was that he had sustained several cracks in his skull. His hands and feet were so grossly disfigured that they were of no use to him. We asked the audience to agree with us in prayer for a miracle, then we anointed him with oil, according to instructions from scripture, placed our hands on his head and prayed.

The miracle came! Immediately his hands and feet were straightened, and he began to run and jump in uncontrolled joy. He was instantly and completely healed by the power of God. I took him, together with his x-rays to the clinic there and new ones confirmed that the injuries were no longer there. This was indeed the greatest discernable miracle I have ever witnessed!

After spending two and one-half years in this, our first pastorate, we resigned the church and once more entered the evangelistic service. This was after the debacle at Pearl Harbor. Many things were rationed, including gasoline. However, in spite of all the obstacles, we were enjoying this phase of our ministry. God blessed us with some outstanding revivals with many people making decisions to serve the Lord.

We traveled from one place to another, closing one revival on Sunday night and starting another on Monday. Our suitcases were hardly ever empty. We took Jimmie Lee's oversized tricycle and a few toys for her. It was a good era of our lives.

Another divine intervention. Broken Arrow was without a pastor. Reverend B. B. Collins, our good friend, was there visiting relatives, and he urged them to contact us. As a result of their pressing invitation, we agreed to stop by for three nights of services on our way to a revival in Arkansas. After preaching those three nights we went on to our revival. We received a telephone call from Doctor Brissey, the church secretary, saying that the wonderful people had elected us 100 percent. After a time of prayer, God confirmed to us that this was His will for us. So, we cancelled our scheduled revivals and moved to the parsonage in Broken Arrow, never imagining that our ministry there would continue for thirty-six years!

We found a small group, about 100 strong, but soon knew that they were some of the finest in the world.

Life was so different when we assumed the pastorate of Broken Arrow in 1942. We had time to visit with our church friends. We became intimately involved in their lives.

Practically everyone died in their home, surrounded with family and friends. We made it a point to be present at their death beds. Francine made a bed in the back seat of our car for the girls, and we sat up with the family all during the night hours, sharing the grief and offering comfort and hope. Then, Francine would hurry by the grocery store and buy a large arm roast. She would surround it with onions, carrots, potatoes and cabbage and have it for their evening meal.

The facilities were nothing to brag about. The church was a little building about fifty feet by fifty feet square, sitting next to the two bedroom parsonage. The church was heated by two large pot-bellied stoves. You were either freezing or sweating. The pews were pine benches. Francine and I would take our hammers and drive down the protruding nails before each service to keep them from tearing women's dresses or men's pants. We didn't mind doing it; we just took that task as part of preparing for the service. The floor was bare of carpet, but we witnessed many a person kneeling at the altars and giving their hearts to God!

I had developed a real closeness with the boys in the church. They were always coming to the parsonage after school and on Saturdays to just hang out. I decided that they needed to have some kind of organization to direct their energies in a way that would make a real difference in each life.

So, I organized "Commandos for Christ." I had real nice patches made for their jackets. We had a special night for meetings. The first part of their meeting was usually football. Then, we all went into the youth chapel for a time of teaching and prayer. This was a serious time of dedicating themselves to the Lord's direction for their lives.

Because of that early foundation, many are now ministers, missionaries, teachers and deacons. They are in the church, participating in choir, orchestra, ushers, etc. They have never wavered. Just to remember brings a sense of blessing and joy to my heart!

In fact, I played football with "my boys" every Saturday morning. They played in our front yard until I eventually obtained the high school football field for such occasions. They were deadly serious with their "play," and as a result, I had regular visits to my optometrist for new lenses.

But the highlight of these meetings was the prayer meetings after each game, where many of them made dedications that have lasted a lifetime.

These were wonderful years. The church was growing. We had respect of the community. The businessmen were all my friends. In fact, many of them requested I preach their funerals and I did.

Our radio ministry actually began with our daily broadcast direct from the living room of the parsonage. Francine played the piano and we sang a song or two. Then I gave a short message. It really surprised me how rapidly it grew into a large listening audience. Then we added a Sunday morning broadcast that aired about the time people would be ready to go to their own church. Bob Eskridge led the choir, and it was real fellowship time as we met early for coffee and rolls. We came on the air singing,

> *Far away in the depths of my spirit today*
>
> *Rings a melody sweeter than song…*
>
> *In celestial like strains it unceasingly rolls*
>
> *O'er my soul like an infinite calm!*

The radio broadcasts brought many friends into our church family. We ministered to shut-ins who had no other church service. Many of the elderly, though we had never met, asked that I preach their funerals. I gladly did … over 3,000 of them during my pastorate there.

We had good rapport with the medical community. All the physicians were my friends, and I saw them often in my calling on their patients in the hospitals. One day, Dr. Franklin, a revered doctor, well known for his dedication to his profession, called me at my study and said, "Pastor, could you please come to my office. I have a lady here who needs you more than she needs me." He introduced her to me and left us alone for our time of prayer. It was my privilege to pray with him in the hospital during his final sickness.

About this time, the government decided to phase out many of the buildings at Camp Gruber. We bought three of the large barracks. I took a group of volunteers from the church, and we demolished the buildings and sent a truck load of lumber back daily. Another crew cleaned the lumber and stacked it in racks, ready for use. Then, for several months, our people worked as a night shift, competing with the hired day workers. In six months, our new, commodious church building was finished and dedicated.

These years were often hectic, long days with little sleep, but they were some of the happiest times of our lives.

Life was so different. Our people were so considerate of their pastor and family. Some of our parishioners were farm people, and they invited me to help myself of all their produce. So, I picked tomatoes, peas, corn, onions, etc. Francine worked late many a night, canning for her family. She not only canned all kinds of vegetables but made chili, catsup, and other wonderful homemade delights. Her pantry was well stocked, and we ate really well! And, many a morning I would go out the front door and find watermelons and cantaloupes.

During this time, we were blessed by the arrival of our second baby girl. Barbara came to delight us. What a happy child! I can still see her, splashing water all over her mother as she bathed her. As soon as she could straighten her little back, she would stand upright in my hand and look all around laughing. She would hold on to a wire and look all around and laugh. What a little show off!

No man ever loved his babies more than I did. I woke them up anytime I came in the house and played with them. My girls are still my most precious possessions.

Another memory: when Barbara could finally run around the house, she considered the phone as part of her personal domain. Anytime it rang, she would out run us to be the first to answer. In her childish voice, she would say, "This is Barbara Dodd a'talkin'." Some people called just to hear her answer the phone.

Our girls were blossoming into beautiful young ladies, winning top awards in school and civic functions. Jimmie Lee won the "Voice of Democracy" contest and was active in school plays. She played her saxophone in the band and starred with her vibraharp in concerts. Barbara was sponsored by the Chamber of Commerce and became Broken Arrow's Junior Miss contestant in the state finals. She won second place in the state. They both represented the city, their church and family in a way we all were always so proud of them. Francine was thoroughly enjoying her responsibilities and was loved by everyone. I was maturing in my ministry to my church, my city, my state and national organization. I was serving as Assistant Superintendent of Oklahoma, was on the Board of Regents for Southwestern University, and member of the General Presbytery Board of the Assemblies of God for life. Life was good!

We got the attention of the whole community and made many friends with the innovations we made. We had large dinners and invited everyone to attend. I bought young buffalo from Lawton, black bear from Minnesota, as well as other unusual items.

Rooster Day with its parade was always a real drawing card for the town. I dressed as the country parson and led the parade in a buggy. We had various floats, representing our children's program, Sunday school, etc. Following our contributions, I had a young man dress as the devil, with placards front and back saying, "Don't attend the Assembly of God Church. They are against me!" That got more attention that I could have anticipated.

One man called my office saying, "Pastor, we'll whip that guy if you'll just tell us to!"

Then the young man himself called, "Pastor, it's getting pretty dangerous down here. I'm in a place of business. Please come up the alley and get me!"

I placed an ad in the Broken Arrow Ledger. It proclaimed in large letters, "Flying saucers will appear over the city at two o'clock Saturday!" Then, together with a pilot friend, we swooped down over Main Street at the appointed time and unloosed a thousand paper saucers. Imprinted on each one was this invitation: "Bring this flying saucer to Sunday school and exchange it for a nice gift!"

Francine was so proud of her family and would have defended any one of them with her life. From her bed, close to the end, she said to me, "I pray for one thing... that all of my family will be with us in heaven!"

Francine, although her health was beginning to disintegrate, was determined to attend all of her grandchildren's weddings. The last one was for Lindsay and Joe Mancuso in Boston. She suffered a severe fall in her hotel room there, but we never heard one complaint from her. She masked any pain she had for fear of dampening the joy of that beautiful occasion. The love she had for her family was absolute.

I was privileged to marry all four of our grandchildren, and she got to attend all of them. I also dedicated all four of our great-grandchildren.

There is:

- Keith Belknap, Jr., is a very successful corporate attorney in Atlanta.

His wife, Jacqueline, has just completed her master's degree in social work (MSW).

- Kimberly Nash and her husband, Bill, are very successful in the music business. They have written songs that have been featured by some of today's most acclaimed artists in their recordings. They also operate, each year, a kid's camp for traumatized kids, free of charge.
- Candice Reid, whose miracle of survival is detailed elsewhere in this book. She has become an outstanding physical therapist in Boston. Her husband, Dave, is tops as a computer wizard.
- Lindsay Mancuso, who will be finishing her college degrees this fall. She has chosen to work with children and is very proficient in that field. Her husband, Joe, who comes from a great family of chefs in Boston, is manager of one of the most favored restaurants in the Boston area.

Now for the great-grandchildren:

- Billy Nash ... a miracle of healing from leukemia as a child. Now a great specimen of manhood whose passion is golf. He certified as a professional golfer.
- Jimmie Nash ... whose one desire is to make his mark in the music world. He is already recording, and we know, with his determination, he will be successful.
- Keith Belknap III ... a gentle giant of a young man, who has the capabilities of succeeding in any area he might choose.
- Christina Belknap ... our youngest great-grandchild and a real sweetheart. She is a happy young lady and is a real joy to all of us. She is in her second year of college.

Here are two of the wonderful miracles in our family ...

First, our little great-grandson, Billy Nash, developed leukemia. We were all devastated and rallied to undergird the parents and grand-parents during this trying time. He was only two years old. The doctors at Texas Children's Hospital in Houston attended him, and we all sent up many prayers for his recovery. His mother, Kim Nash, stayed in his room constantly, keeping an open Bible on the bed, continually reading God's provision for healing. She refused to allow anyone in the room who would speak negatively about his recovery. Mom and I spent many weeks there, taking some of the responsibilities. His grandmother, Jimmie, never left him at all until his marvelous return to health. It was indeed heartbreaking to see the little fellow suffer so much from the terrible treatments.

But we saw the intervention of God as he began to recover. A friend of his dad had given him a complete drum set, and he would play it for hours, oblivious to everyone around him, finding comfort from his medical condition.

God answered prayer. He is now a living specimen of divine health. He stands over six feet tall and weighs almost 200 pounds. Upon his recovery, the Leukemia Association asked him to represent their cause and he still does it gladly. He goes into the wards of that great hospital and tells his story. What a blessing to burdened parents as they see hope for their children. His photo graces the hall of the leukemia ward; he speaks every summer at a youth camp, sponsored by his parents for children who have experienced trauma in their lives. Every child is welcomed and there is no charge. In his file in Texas Children's Hospital he is a documented miracle. There it is in black and white.

As a note of interest, he has been certified as a professional golfer.

Our phone rang in the middle of the night. It had an ominous sound. We were shocked and horrified by the news. Our grandchild, Candice Nicholle, had been involved in an accident and her very life hung in the balance.

She had gone, with her fiancé, Dave Reid, to a friend's house there in Chicago. Dave guided her out on the third floor balcony. The balcony collapsed and they were flung down the three stories. Candice landed on an outside grill. Her neck was broken in two places, and her body sustained other terrible injuries. Dave had a broken shoulder. While getting ready to catch the first available plane, we turned on the TV. The accident was already shown on the national news, and we saw them taking her bloodied and broken body to the trauma hospital.

We arrived as soon as the airline could take us and met her mother, Barbara, waiting anxiously for us. In another part of Chicago, our grandson, Keith Belknap had heard the news and had hurried to the hospital. He was an encouragement. He was a member of her family.

It was agonizing to see her poor, broken body. She was on a special trauma bed, and no one was allowed to even touch the bed. They had not been able to clean away the blood. Though I could not touch her wounded body, I stood beside her and asked God for a miracle.

The next day, I had a conversation with the trauma specialist who was constantly attending her. He said to me, "Reverend, this girl should be dead, but she isn't. If not dead, she should be completely paralyzed ... but she isn't." He continued, "It's beyond understanding."

Then began the slow process of recovery. Barbara was with her day and night, and when she could eventually be released, she took Candice home with her to Connecticut and nursed her back to health.

When she was finally able to travel by plane, she called me one day and asked, "Papa, I need to talk to you, can I come and see you this next Sunday?" Of course, I was delighted to have her come.

Candice had been very successful in the insurance business. She had the company car and all the benefits. It seemed her future was secure.

But she sat in our living room and the tears began to come. Then she said, "Papa, I need your advice. I know that I'm a miracle. I'm thinking of changing the course of my life. I want to be in a vocation where I can help people who go through traumas like I experienced. I want to go into the field of physical therapy. I have been blessed by my wonderful therapists, and it has given me a desire to be one. I know it will require a lot of me, and of Dave, too, but my spirit urges me on ... what do you advise me to do?"

Without hesitation I replied, "Honey, if God has laid this on your heart, go for it. He will bless your dedication, and you'll be a great one!"

So she did, and she is.

God gave us many outstanding friends.

Dr. Oral Roberts, his wife Evelyn, and his family were good friends. I was welcomed to their farm to ride horses with Oral and to just enjoy looking at the fabulous cattle he had at his ranch. Evelyn and the children attended our worship service on Sunday mornings when Oral was away. He always attended, when possible, when we had our mutual friend, Vep Ellis, in special services. He sent us a generous offering after our church was destroyed by fire. I was a guest speaker at chapel. When I was district superintendent and was not well for awhile, he called at my office and prayed with me. I will never forget that act of love! Oral's dear wife, Evelyn, is now in heaven. I'm sure she and Francine have renewed friendships.

Dr. T.L. and Daisy Osborne held us a revival and continued attending our Sunday morning services. I visited with them in their Tulsa headquarters many times. I was also guest speaker for their chapel services.

Senator Bob Kerr's office called to set up an appointment with me in his Tulsa office. He was very gracious and gave me a check for $10,000 to help with our rebuilding the church after it was destroyed by fire.

Mr. Mabee, who at that time owned Braden Winch Company in Broken Arrow, had his secretary set up a meeting with me in the parking lot of the winch company. I arrived first, and he drove up soon in an old model pickup. He came to my car and gave me a check for $10,000.

Sheriff Dave Faulkner counted on our ladies, headed by Cora Bowles, to serve lunch every time his political parades came anywhere near Broken Arrow. He was also a true friend of mine. He would send one of his deputies to my office every time he needed a new deputy in the Broken Arrow area, asking for a recommendation of a good man for the job.

One day his office called and asked me to meet the sheriff in his office. When I arrived, he and his deputies were all present. They presented me with a written declaration, naming me a Tulsa County Deputy Sheriff, with all the privileges of such office. Then, they pinned on me a deputy sheriff's badge, the real thing, a gold badge naming "James C. Dodd, Tulsa County Deputy Sheriff." A Tulsa police officer brought me a new five shot Derringer, which I still have but have never fired a shot from.

The businessmen of our city, without exception, were my friends. Regardless of their church affiliation, many of them came to my study for counsel. They attended and supported our church dinners, helped sponsor our radio broadcasts. Several of them asked me to preach their funerals. I did so, going to their own churches for the service.

As I look back on my early years, one thing stands out... I was always taking chances. I craved excitement, even if I had to manufacture it myself. That desire seemed to follow me, and it showed up, even in my pastoral years, in my personal life and financial endeavors.

Francine had a wonderful class of teenage girls. They were having a party in their upstairs classroom. I thought I'd give the young ladies a surprise visit. So I obtained one of Francine's silk hose, pulled it down over my face and, opening the door a little, just looked in on them. When they glimpsed that hideous face, they stampeded! The rout was on. They jostled one another. The end result was one girl had a chipped tooth and another wet herself. I was apologetic and embarrassed. I had some fences to mend with my wife and everyone involved. I had no idea of this turn of events.

Did I learn my lesson? Sadly, I did not. Francine's mom was visiting us. She was very nervous as the night was stormy, with thunder rolling and lightning flashing and the rain coming down. I raided the hosiery drawer, slipped around the house. Just as Mom looked anxiously through the open window, lightning flashed, and I looked in at her.

She had the same result as did the young lady in the class. When I went back inside I thought she was intent on beating me to death! It took awhile for us to become friends again.

Francine and I were hosting the youth group in the fellowship hall. I was preparing my own version of "dogs on a stick." I had prepared ahead and had a big rubber wiener. I rolled it in the batter and put it in the fryer and it came out perfect. I gave it to a young man who was always pulling jokes on others. He bit down on the dog but could not penetrate it. Looking so perplexed, he tried again and again while everyone enjoyed his efforts. Finally, he pulled it apart and joined in the laughter. He is now a pastor in South Carolina, and I'm very proud of him!

I often scribbled little pieces of poetry for Francine. She kept them all and here are a couple, the first one in 1968, on our thirty-third wedding anniversary:

Only thirty-three years ago today
We took the awesome leap
A boy and girl so much in love
We didn't fear the waters deep.
The years have quickly come and gone
Along the path of life
So many things have made me glad
That I took Francie for my wife.
Today we pause and look around
Upon the blessings of our Lord
Our life together has been great
We've proved the truth of His good word.
We thank Him for His love and favor
For all the things which we possess
But of the stockpile of the years
The things material are the less.
Jimmie came to bless our home
Then Barbara came to beguile
Two little girls just right for us
They made our lives worthwhile.
So, now we face a future bright
For we walk hand in hand
We'll walk together, still in love
'Till we come to that good land.
And when at last the call shall come
To heaven's lovely weather
We'll be at home and wait until
Our family 'round us gather!"

I wrote this to Francine on the occasion of our thirty-ninth anniversary:

Thirty-nine years ago
In a town called Seminole
A little teenage girl in brown
Who didn't own a wedding gown
Said, "Yes!" to the parson's son
Thinking life would all be fun.

JAMES C. DODD

The years have fled away
And here they stand today
She still has that girlish figure
And he still says, "I dig her!"
They're not afraid of the passing years
For they've shared so many smiles and tears.
To him she's his little girl in brown
Who never owned a wedding gown
But she had worth beyond compare
She shaped his life and did her share
To build a home full and complete
A life so full it could never be beat!

There are unknown forces in this world that change us irrevocably, without our being conscious of it. Such was the era of World War II, Vietnam, and Korea. Many of our young men from the church were involved. Three of them paid the ultimate price with their lives.

I was liaison for the Red Cross for our community during this time. It was my responsibility to go to the homes and inform them of the death of their son or husband. It was a hard task, and I grieved with every family thus involved. At times, I would go to the depot with the family and undertaker to meet the train carrying their loved one home. We would place the coffin on a gurney and take it to the funeral home. I can still see the anguish of wives and mothers as they embraced the coffin that held the fallen soldier … war enacts a terrible price on everyone involved!

We never made a charge to the bereaved for my services or for the use of the church when people lost a loved one.

Our ministry was not only to our church body but to the community in many ways.

One of the main streets of town was blocked off to traffic every Saturday night for our street meeting. Literally hundreds of people made it part of their weekly endeavor to participate … some who would not enter a church building were there to enjoy the open air ministry.

We began to publish a monthly magazine, done professionally, and sent it free to every home in town and to all the rural routes. It began to have a positive effect.

To undergird our radio ministry, we had a "Radio Banquet" annually. Many hundreds came in addition to our own members. We served a fantastic dinner in the school cafeteria. And the end result was that every broadcast for the coming year was fully sponsored.

I started a "Dial-A-Message" from my study. I could hear the machine responding to calls day and night.

While pastoring at Broken Arrow, I was appointed to serve on various boards and committees at the national level. This entailed my spending time in Springfield, Missouri, at our headquarters. I well remember one such trip.

I had flown in late one day to be present at the meeting of our mission committee. I had checked in at the hotel which had motel like rooms also. I requested a room at the very backside as I was tired and wanted to have a quiet room to catch a good night's rest. I had bathed, put on my robe and laid down on the bed.

Suddenly, I heard a commotion at the back entrance to my room. Someone was kicking the door in. I only had time to jump up and open the glass door that led out to the swimming pool. As I stood there the door splintered and my assailant fell in, on top of the door, right before me.

I was standing there quietly, nothing with which to defend myself. Then the intruder looked at me, a look of horror on his face, as he twisted around and ran away as fast as he could go. I knew this man was not afraid of me as I stood helplessly by in my robe, nothing in my hand. I will always believe that an angel from God was there and he saw him. This feeling was compounded as I went with the police to the station and identified him from their photos. He was a several times convicted felon, known for his strong-arm robberies.

I was made to thank God for His covering and protection for His people, even when they are not aware of His presence. I include this in this book to give testimony to and praise to Him!

I wrote a column for the *Broken Arrow Ledger,* and it was carried on the front page of the paper.

I have always believed that the Sunday school is the lifeblood of the church. We entered a nationwide Sunday school contest sponsored by *Christian Life* magazine (Robert Walker, editor). We won first prize in our category every year.

A young businessman, who happened to be my Sunday School Superintendent, designed and built an entire miniature train for a Sunday school project we came up with. It was complete, from the engine to the caboose, with as many various cars as we had Sunday school classes. The positions for the cars depended on the percentage of gain over the previous Sunday. This created a lot of friendly competition. Everyone wanted to be the engine and no one wanted to be the caboose. The train looked very authentic. This little train became somewhat famous and was featured at the state and national Sunday school conventions!

One week, I obtained a list of absentees as soon as Sunday school was over. I had a contingent of young people on bicycles to deliver subpoenas to each absentee, requesting their appearance next Sunday at 9:45 a.m.!

We challenged several nationally known churches to a six-week attendance contest. The churches were located in California, Missouri, and Arkansas. We called them right after the Sunday school each week and announced our standing in the morning worship time.

We also entered the National Sunday School Attendance Contest, sponsored by *Christian Life* magazine and won first place in our category every year.

During these years of growth, we sometimes ran out of space. So, we rented tents and had a "tent city" surrounding our church. It was a sign to the city that this church was alive and well and outgrowing our facilities.

My idea was and is that no amount of planning and effort is too big a price to pay to see unchurched people come to a saving knowledge of our blessed Lord!

Any property on our block or adjacent to it was bought as soon as it came on the market. We needed room for expansion.

We had many of the great Gospel quartets as guests. Among those quartets who were our guests were "The Statesmen." They sang for us the Sunday morning before our church was destroyed by fire that night.

Then there were "The Galileans," "The Stamps-Baxter Quartet," and everyone's all-time favorite, "The Speer Family." The Speers sang often on Sunday afternoon at the convention center in Tulsa. Brock would call me and say that they could be with us on Sunday night. We were always ready to say yes!

I had served the Oklahoma District Council as Assistant Superintendent for over thirty years, and now they asked me to assume the superintendency. I had some praying to do before accepting. And I had to consider Francine's feelings about it. You see, I had bought her a lovely home in Tulsa. This home was owned by a Jewish heart specialist who practiced primarily at St. Francis Hospital. He had a lovely wife who formerly was married to one of our ministers. He was killed in a plane crash as he sought to minister in the area where we had later gone. She later married this famous doctor. The house was to be sold by sealed bids, so I entered ours and waited for the result.

It turned out that someone else had bid $5,000 more than my bid, and the doctor was about to accept his bid. Then the power of a good wife came into play. She emphatically declared, "No sir, you will not accept that offer . . . the preacher's going to get this house!" At the closing, he laughingly said, "Can you imagine, me a Jew, taking $5,000 less than I could have received?"

We moved in and had some happy months there; Francine loved the place and had furnished it with a lot of new furniture. So I sought out her feelings about us selling it so soon. I'll never forget her immediate answer: "Honey, you know I love this house, but it is only a house. I have trusted you to follow the leading of the Lord all these years and now if you feel this move is in the will of God for us, I am ready!" That confirmed it for me and I accepted the invitation.

While superintendent, I started "P.K. Retreat," a wonderful camping experience for all the teenagers of our ministers' families. This consisted of a week's supervised event at our beautiful, air-conditioned youth camp. Everything was absolutely free and was a fun time as well as a worshipful experience.

Our present District Superintendent, Rev. Frank Cargill, at that time was our District Youth Leader. So I thought it consistent that I enlist him and his wife, Linda, in this new venture. The results were outstanding and "P.K. Retreat" has been an annual event ever since. Meeting a crying need in the lives of these young people, who too often are subjected to temptations and rebuffs that are not common to others.

So, we bought a lovely home in Edmond, the prime residential area in Oklahoma City suburbs. We spent three and a half years in that position before my health made me think about moving Francine back where she had a lot of close friends. My prognosis at that time made me think that this was the wise thing to do.

But, that period of time was one of the busiest and happiest periods of our lives. I had 850 churches and 1,500 ministers in my jurisdiction.

Francine took to this big adjustment and enjoyed every phase of it. She was indeed Oklahoma's "First Lady." She went with me to all the sectional, state, and national meetings. Everyone loved her, and with her there was no such thing as "big preachers" or "little preachers." She loved them and their families all alike. I honestly believe that there was no one in the entire district council to whom she did not give a friendly hug and words of encouragement.

Francine adored all of her family, but she seemed to have a special love for her brother, Colombus P., better known to all his friends as "Lum." He returned that special affection. He called every night to talk awhile and to see how she was. When we accepted the superintendency of the Oklahoma district, it required us to travel all over the state and also nationally. He expressed his disfavor with this by saying to her, "I thought surely, at your age, you would settle down and I wouldn't have to worry so much about you. But, you are on the go all the time and I never know where to call you."

He was her confidante, and she enjoyed every attention he gave her.

In preparation for our moving back, I bought a 5,200 square foot home on the eleventh green at Cedar Ridge Country Club. It was indeed a real work of art, complete with everything that would make life pleasant, including a great Jacuzzi. We thoroughly enjoyed its many amenities. Francine delighted in making huge dinners there for her family. We spent many an evening on the large patio watching the golfers, and, we had free entrance to all the world-class championships played there.

We, of course, had access to the club dining facilities, where we entertained our family and friends. I think we missed that part more than anything else when we moved away.

We lived in that wonderful house for ten years, but as we grew older, it became too big for us. We regretfully sold it and bought a 3,500 square foot home off of South Yale on Toledo Avenue. It was a beautiful home, situated on a corner lot with magnificent landscaping. We had almost another ten years of happiness in that home and wonderful neighbors who became great friends.

All through my ministry, I have loved studying the Word of God. In fact, right after accepting my first pastorate at Glad Tidings in Shawnee, I began consistently going through courses of study. I spent many hours, late at night, pouring over assignments, etc., and completed the requirements for ministerial recognition. In addition to my own Assemblies of God courses, I completed, by correspondence from a famous school in Chicago, my doctorate. I have never been anxious to use it attached to my name. My main purpose was to learn, the other was incidental.

In 1994, Bob Burke published his highly acclaimed book *"Like a Prairie Fire," A History of the Assemblies of God in Oklahoma.* Our ministry was included a number of times. We include a few excerpts as it catalogues some highlights that will give a glimpse of our ministry and of our theological and psychological beliefs.

First, he mentions our first church: "Glad Tidings Assembly" in Shawnee, Oklahoma, had its beginning in November, 1939. "Soon, young James and Francine Dodd became pastors of the church, Brother Dodd called Raymond T. Richey, (one of the most sought after evangelists in the Assemblies of God) to hold his first revival. The civic auditorium was rented for the ten day meeting that drew crowds as large as 6,000. Songwriter Ira Stanphil was the song leader!"

Then, he quoted from a message I preached at the Oklahoma District Council: "We have crossed the threshold of a new era. Our western civilization is at the crossroads ... ideologies are crashing about us ... there is an increasing tendency to gloss over the awfulness of sin, to condone and compromise. There is a disregard for the work of the individual ... our nation has a rendezvous with destiny. It is a question of world revival or world catastrophe ... the Holy Ghost has been grieved out of many churches. People will file into the pews with broken hearts, burdened souls, tormented lives, doubts, fears, hesitations. The only message that will help them is the message of the Lamb of God ... we cannot fulfill our mission by criticizing the modernist, finding fault with our fellows, blaming juvenile delinquency, saying that our churches are worldly ... I believe in separation, but separation is not enough. We must demonstrate to a lost world what it means to be indwelt by the Spirit!"

On page 374: "When Dodd was elected Sectional Presbyter, he was the youngest preacher in district history to ever serve in that position. Since he was raised in a pastor's home, he had a special compassion for older ministers. His District Superintendent's Column in *The Assemblies of God News* in January, 1983, was a glowing tribute to pioneer preachers: 'I stand in awe at their dedication. They went anywhere a door opened— brush arbors, country schoolhouses, street corners. They established churches in homes, in empty store fronts, anywhere. They lived on meager incomes. They endured persecutions that most of us know nothing about. And now, some of those valiant old warriors are almost forgotten. They sit at home alone, with their memories. No doubt they close their eyes and remember the crowds, the altars filled with sinners coming to God, the Sunday dinners with some of the saints, the recognition as a man of God ... let us not be guilty of delegating, by our neglect our worthy forbears to a bare existence while we fare sumptuously!'"

Note: After recording the New Testament on tape, I took them to a convention where I was the speaker, and they bought $30,000 worth of them. I brought the entire amount back and gave it to the District Treasurer to be placed in the Aged Ministers Fund. It gave me great pleasure to do that.

I've been asked the question, "Rev. Dodd, will you, in layman's terms tell us some of the truths you believe and cling to? Speak of your beliefs that you feel are so intrinsically a part of you that there is no room for compromise."

First, let us establish that the Bible, in its entirety, is forever and always, unchanging, the Word of God to man. Scoffers may arise and skeptics argue, but the Word stands as a rock of Gibraltar, and will be the basis for judgment at the Judgment Seat of Christ. God is so zealous for His Word that He declares in Revelation 22:18–19, "For I testify unto every man that heareth the words of the book of this prophecy, if any man shall add unto these things, God will add unto him the plagues that are written in this book: and if any man shall take away from the words of the book of this prophecy, God shall take away his part out of the Book of Life and out of the holy city, and from the things which are written in this book."

Second, salvation is the free gift of God; it is not achieved by good works, it is taken by faith. I believe in the altar as a place of repentance. The altar can be any place where we acknowledge our sins, ask forgiveness and arise to "walk in newness of life." Sin cuts its merciless swath through the entire human race, not missing a single human heart. In the end, we must acknowledge the darkness within us and the light that comes only from God. Every atom of our bodies is infected by the disease of sin, but every atom may likewise be covered by the grace of God. The vilest offender can be covered by the grace of God and reap the deepest joys of heaven!

Third, I rejoice that the precious Holy Spirit is sent from heaven to inhabit the lives of the redeemed. I speak of that definite experience that comes to the believer after salvation and is accompanied by speaking in other tongues as the Spirit gives utterance. Then, after this initial experience, there are different manifestations and gifts that follow.

Oh, how comforting is His leading us to speak in our heavenly language in our private prayer life.

He uses individuals, who are filled with the Spirit and open to His direction to speak forth in the congregation to bless and to edify His saints.

I have witnessed, time and again, the Spirit of God sweep over an entire congregation in response to a message and interpretation from an obedient child of God. We can no more confine or limit His working to our limited way of thinking than we can harness the wind. "The wind bloweth where it listeth!" Where the Holy Spirit is welcomed He will make known His presence. We have warning from Scripture in Ephesians 4:30, "And grieve not the Holy Spirit of God, whereby you are sealed unto the day of redemption."

Divine healing ... I have experienced it again and again in my ministry. I can document absolute miracles in my own life and in countless lives of others. The enemy tried to cut my life short toward the very beginning of my ministry. Four of us drank from a well and contracted typhoid fever. Three wound up as hospital patients. One man died, and I spent weeks lingering between life and death. I lost 100 pounds. Then, a group of young people fasted and prayed, and I was restored. Later in my ministry, I was sidelined by a malignant lymphoma. The cancer specialist gave me a thirty percent chance for recovery. But God! I have been free of that plague for over seven years! "By His stripes we are healed!" So wonderful!

I am expecting Jesus to "come again" any time soon. Acts 1:11 " ... ye men of Galilee, why stand ye gazing up into heaven? This same Jesus, which is taken up from you into heaven, shall so come again in like manner as ye have seen Him go into heaven!"

What a day that will be! The trumpet sounding! Graves of the righteous dead erupting! Tombstones scattered in disarray! Reunions in the sky! Death's sorrow replaced with joy unspeakable and full of glory! "So Christ was once offered to bear the sins of many; and unto them that look for Him shall He appear the second time without sin unto salvation" Hebrews 9:28.

My girls were always close to their daddy. Recently they both wrote me a letter. I choose to share it with you as it really speaks of that closeness that has been there down through the years ...

Dear Daddy,

On this Father's Day, I'm thinking of some of my favorite memories of my daddy and me.

I remember the grocery store and how much fun it was as my dog, "Brownie," and I romped and played in it. I remember going with you on deliveries. You would let me sit on top of the box of groceries and carry me in on them.

I remember one delivery. I was standing behind your right shoulder and you drove that T-model delivery truck around a corner too fast and the door came open. I went sailing out but you caught me by my ankle and saved me. You've "saved" me many times since!

I remember Christmas at Grandma and Grandpa's. I was so excited to see all my cousins because I was still an only child. The bad part was that Santa Claus would always show up in full dress and a long, white beard. The other kids would laugh and jump around. I would hide my face in Mother's lap and scream until Santa left. I begged Daddy to never let him come again. On his last visit, I cried and said, "If he's coming back I hope I die first!" You know that was the last time he showed himself. My cousins forgave me as the presents still came.

I remember the new bike you brought home to me. I would ride all over the lawn in front of the church and parsonage with you holding on to the back fender, running to keep up with me. I finally got good enough for you to just lay your hand on the back of the fender and run along behind. I would keep looking back and if you had moved your hand I would fall. Such is the power of a father's guiding hand!

I want you to know how much I admire you and how proud I am of the man you are. Our family has such a blessed heritage! I am so thankful for the love and the example of this truly wonderful man my children and grandchildren have from watching your life and feeling your unconditional love.

I love you, my sweet daddy, and it is an honor to be your daughter!

Love,

Jimmie

Proverbs 14:26

JAMES C. DODD

Father's Day...

Dad, just thinking about some of our times together.

I will never forget the ritual of you and I locking up the church after everyone had left. We usually started by locking the front door, turning off the row of switches that controlled all of the auditorium lights, then we climbed the flight of stairs to the top floor to check the fire escape door and turn off all the upstairs lights. Usually by that time you would tell me to go ahead and check the basement while you finished up in the office. Starting at the far end, I would cautiously, yet quickly as possible, make sure all the lights were off and doors locked. About at this point I would start breathing fast in anticipation of what was to come—the dead heat run for my life. As a pastor's child, I heard all the stories and speculations of people hiding in the church or in the attic to spend the night. Unfortunately, the only light switch to the main floor hall lights was at the end of the hall. I would take a deep breath, turn off the light and run as fast as I could to your office door, feeling the church ghosts and the overnight uninvited guests breathing down the back of my neck. Of course, when I walked into your office, I acted as if I didn't have a care in this world. You were the bravest person I could imagine, and I wanted to be that way too, at least in your eyes.

While you were in your study, working out a sermon, I would sneak around the side of the church and climb those shaky stairs to the fire escape. From there, I found a ledge that I could scale to inch around the side of the church overlooking our neighbor's corn patch. As the gusts of Oklahoma wind almost took me as well as the high stalks of corn, I would demand (in God's name of course), "Peace be still!" I would yell it out over and over until the wind took a pause. For some reason, I never doubted even when the wind would rise again, that was all the reassurance needed to energize me as that was after all proof that I was speaking God's command! In that moment, calming the seas of corn felt equal to preaching a sermon like my dad... almost!

I happened upon a picture of you preaching on a Sunday morning and at your side at the pulpit much to my surprise was guess who... me! I must have been about four years of age. I wasn't surprised that I would want to be there but that you treated it as normal and allowed it. No wonder your words have found such a lodging place in my heart and mind.

I will never forget how music was such a part of our lives. Mother would sing hymns as she went about her housework or when playing with me. And later with her grandchildren. You kept us all singing for a major part of every service. Sometimes when the church windows were open, I could hear you whistling as I played in the yard and it always made my heart smile.

As I grew older it was my job to explore God's message, and your words, as well as your approach to religion, to worship, and to life. Sometimes I agreed and sometimes I disagreed, but never veered too far away. How could I? Of course as I grew older and you and Mother shared more, you proved that you were human like the rest of us. All parents should do that. When children know more about the hard times or those times when their parents needed God's hand to reach down and lift them up, then a new understanding of God's grace is allowed to flow from one generation to the next. By your example, you and Mother planted God's seeds of truth and love and hope deep within your children.

I just wanted to thank you on this Father's Day for thousands of experiences that fed my spirit, my outlook on life, and the way I have parented. I have been blessed with such fabulous children and their strengths can be traced back from generation to generation.

Your daughter, Barbara, with a lot of love

On the occasion of our fiftieth wedding anniversary, our girls, Jimmie and Barbara, went "all out" to give us a most precious gift. They had the church sanctuary and the fellowship hall all banked with the most gorgeous flowers. A harpist was playing in a gazebo in the middle of the court. All kinds of refreshments were served. Several hundred friends shared the evening with us, including all the Oklahoma District officials.

After a rededication ceremony in the auditorium, everyone went to the court for photos, friendship and food.

What a beautiful evening! Francine was so happy, and she looked so beautiful in the new evening dress I bought for her in Houston. It all made up for the very simple wedding we had fifty years earlier!

Two of our close friends, Rev. Tom Goins and Dr. Armon Newburn officiated at the renewing of our vows ceremony.

Our young people always had a large refreshment stand on "Rooster Day." We had more business than any other stand, because we featured my invention of dogs on a stick and Jim Holder's "Rooster Juice." These were happy times, making friends and seeing the church grow. We were the largest Assemblies of God Church in Oklahoma and were winning national awards for Sunday school attendance.

Then the unthinkable happened. The city's night watchman pounded on my door and cried, "Pastor, the church is on fire!"

This was the largest fire Broken Arrow had ever witnessed. Fire departments from Tulsa responded to assist our volunteer forces. It was a devastating experience. This happened on Sunday night, after we had just set the all-time record of 937 that very day. We won the national Sunday school contest that month, sponsored by *Christian Life* magazine, and they carried a picture of the blazing fire on their front cover.

But the spirit of our people met the challenge. Before the ashes were cool, bulldozers were clearing away the debris and another, bigger and better building was begun.

Because of the sacrificial spirit of our people and their dedication to the work of rebuilding, we built this beautiful church back in another six months' time. A little later, we added a large gymnasium along with offices, snack bar, and book store. We enjoyed these facilities through the remaining years of our pastorate. All this time our ministry was evolving and taking on more responsibilities. I was serving as Assistant Superintendent of the state, a General Presbyter to our national organization, a member of the Board of Regents for our Southwestern University in Waxahachie, Texas, along with various other committees and boards.

Our church was very missions oriented. As a result, Francine and I began to travel overseas to enjoy commitments in many countries and in diverse circumstances and cultures.

I took several preaching appointments when she could not accompany me because of family. I spent three days in Stockholm, Sweden, at the world conference. Then, on to Paris, where I preached three times on a Sunday in three different auditoriums. A wonderful time of blessing followed as I ministered for ten nights in our great church in Lisbon, Portugal. Then, after arriving back in the states, a convention in Canada. I also took my first holy land trip. I was gone for three weeks and got to see and do a lot of things that are no longer available to anyone.

For example, I climbed Mount Sinai and preached at the very top in the place where Moses received the commandments directly from God. I ministered on "the two mountains … Sinai and Calvary." I still am blessed with this memory!

I was a guest at the centuries old monastery, located at the foot of the mountain. Absolutely no one is allowed in there now. The monastery is built around a shrub that they claimed was the original "burning bush." An old monk invited me to take a tour of the cellar area. It was the most amazing scene I had ever witnessed. For centuries the old monks lived and died there at Saint Catherine's Monastery. At death, they were buried in a shallow grave and then, after two years had passed, they were dug up and their skeletons were pulled apart and stored in this huge cellar. They stacked the arms in one pile, legs in another, and a huge stack of skulls filled one corner. This was that they might completely lose their identity.

This was such a closed society that they did not even have a front door. They lowered a rope from the window, located in the second floor and pulled you up by that means.

After looking over those huge piles of the remains of the centuries of dedicated men, I remarked to my host, "I'd sure like to be here on resurrection morning."

He replied, "Why would you like that?"

"Oh," I replied, "When God's trumpet sounds these bones are going to come together!" I don't think he had ever heard of such a thing.

After this experience, I determined that I wanted to share these wonderful events with my wife. Jimmie Lee was now married and Barbara was thirteen, old enough to take on the hardships that just naturally came with some of the trips. So, we were off to Italy. What a blessed experience. Accompanied by our interpreter, Rev. Alred Perna, we traveled down the boot, preaching every day to a different audience. This was before the country had real religious liberty, and we ministered in cellars, churches carved out of solid rock, etc. There were four of us crowded into a little Fiat, with luggage strapped on top of the car. I especially enjoyed ministering in Andria, one of the two towns where we had built churches for the impoverished people. They had been worshipping in a cow barn. We built them a beautiful church, complete with chandeliers, etc. The men all sat on one side of the church and the women sat on the other side. The women were so excited that we were there, that they were really buzzing with conversation. The old pastor went back and rebuked them saying, "The Bible says for the women to keep silent in the church and if they want to know anything, let them ask their husband at home." After service, they each one came to the pastor and asked his forgiveness. I'm sure, if this had happened in the states, it would have been a different outcome. In another larger town, Toronto, we bought a movie theatre and turned it into a church. Under the leadership of a young minister and his wife, it is now the largest evangelical church in Italy. We could fill up many pages, telling how God worked and gave us tremendous results.

We found Rome to be one of the most enchanting cities we visited. In addition to the thrill of preaching several times in our great church there, we took in the famous sights and scenes. We ate lunch at a wonderful café just across from the beautiful fountain made famous by the song "Three Coins in the Fountain," admired the Vatican with its famous Michelangelo frescoes and paintings, saw the oldest church in the world, explored the coliseum where many of the early Christians were martyred, climbed Martin Luther's long stairway of penance where now many devout Catholics go up on their knees, stood reverently in the little rock hewn cell where the Apostle Paul spent many months alone but witnessed daily to his guards and whoever else came his way. We were staying at a little, out-of-the way pension until Rev. Perna, our interpreter and guide, came and removed us to his home, where Mrs. Perna regaled us daily with wonderful several course dinners. She was always saying, "Brother Dodd, you're going to lose weight." I had just eaten so much I could hardly move. In fact, she put such helpings on my plate, I secretly moved some of it from my plate to Al Junior's. He was a growing teenager and gladly consumed any and all of my offerings.

We went out from home to see the devastated city of Pompeii and Mount Vesuvius. The sinful city of Pompeii, known all over the then known world for its debauchery and unrestrained living, was completely bereft of every human soul when Mount Vesuvius erupted in 79 A.D. The eruption of ash was so sudden and complete that the inhabitants had no chance to flee. Their suffocated bodies, completely encased in ash, can be seen today. What an example of God's wrath.

We went on to Mount Vesuvius and actually walked across the top. The ground would give under our feet and little flames of fire would come through the surface. There was one place that was called "The Gate to Hell." Fire roared out of the crevice unceasingly. What a graphic picture!

From Rome, we took a midnight flight across the Sahara Desert to Kano, the mud city of Nigeria. It was a seat-buckled flight. We could only get two tickets for coach so we bought one first class and put Barbara in that one. As the old British Airways jet was really rolling, I thought I should make my way up front and check on Barbara. She was sitting, apparently, completely composed, watching some of the other passengers with their "whoopee" cups.

After a few days of ministry there, we flew on to Monrovia, Liberia. What a thrilling time we had in that country. As we had pre-arranged business to conduct with President Tubman, Barbara and I were guests at his country estate. As I explained to him about a certain condition that was hampering our missionaries in their labors, he called for his secretary and dictated the solution to our problems while I was still in the room. I then presented him with the finest Thompson Chain Reference Bible, red in color, with his name and position as President inscribed on it. Then, he took Barbara by the hand and escorted us through his private zoo. I have often wished that Francine could have shared this experience with us. She had stayed behind in Monrovia to rest and to minister to the mission wives as only she could.

Then, we traveled inland by pick-up truck to minister in the leper colony. We rode in the back of the pick-up surrounded by lepers. They were very careful not to touch us. This colony was known and famous throughout Africa. Our missionary lady, "Ma" Steidel, had built the clinic there. The President, in recognition of her sacrifices, deeded several hundred acres of jungle to our mission, and the Firestone Rubber Company planted hundreds of rubber trees for us. The lepers collected the rubber, and the colony became self-supporting. We kept two RN ladies there to minister to the needs of the lepers. The leper families lived with their afflicted member while treatment was ongoing.

We settled into one of the mission homes and began our preaching to the lepers. I preached every day at 7:00 a.m. and again at 7:00 p.m. They all were there for every service and many of them gave their hearts to the Lord. I know we will see some of them in heaven. Barbara had a congregation of her own. She would sit on the lawn of the mission house, and every child in the compound would sit around her listening to Bible stories. She also apparently had an affinity with the little chimps and most of the time, one would be hanging on her neck. For some reason they hated me, and I had to keep away from them.

It would fill a whole book to recite all the experiences we had there. One day a young man came to me and said, "Pa, you come with me, and I'll show you two lions. You shoot 'em!" I declined his invitation.

Again, a black mamba cobra was killed in the girls' outside toilet.

Francine loved the bananas they grew there in the jungle. We could buy a whole stalk for twenty-five cents. She ate them for breakfast and at various times all through the day. And, I can still see her, seated on the platform, clapping her hands in unison with the beat from the makeshift orchestra.

Mrs. Steidel was losing her health as a result of the many years of loving service to her beloved lepers. We brought her out with us for medical treatment when we finally left Africa.

Preaching to the lepers was one of the greatest thrills of my ministry. While in the leper colony on a later trip, our daughter, Jimmie Lee, was attacked by soldier ants and was bitten 110 times. She had to undergo months of intensive treatment upon her return to Tulsa.

We stopped at Plebo on our way to our next appointment. Francine and Barbara stayed with a couple of lady missionaries. I stayed with the missionary family across the valley. There was a large native village in the valley between us. You could hear them singing, playing their crude instruments and dancing all night long.

I slept in the attic. The furniture was a single bed, draped with mosquito netting. I slept well, although I did hear some little animals moving around. After returning home, I got a letter from the missionary saying, "After you left we discovered a large black mamba spitting cobra in the attic. We killed it." Thank God for the protection we receive, unknowingly, from the precious Holy Spirit!

We moved on to Accra, Ghana, where we again witnessed the hand of God on our journey. I was honored to preach in the great church in Accra.

A couple of our missionaries approached me, saying, "We have discovered a tribe far back in the interior who have just one time heard the good news of the Gospel. We are going to trek back in there for another preaching mission and will take you if you want to go!" I gladly accepted. Although I was completely unprepared for the experience.

We went by car until the roads ran out and then began our walking into the jungle. After what seemed hours, we knew we were nearing our destination. We could hear singing and beating of drums. Suddenly, we saw them coming up the trail to meet us. They were singing "Here comes the king!" Then a large native man, with nothing on but a breach cloth, stepped out in front with a coconut and machete in his hand. While holding the coconut in one hand, he struck it with three blows and the top was removed. He handed it to me to drink the milk. It was really refreshing after the long trek through the dense jungle.

As we went farther, we could see the whole tribe gathered on the side of the hill. And, just below them, was a small arbor where the king sat. The large village pot was bubbling with the soup of the day. Two women, completely undressed down to their waists, were pounding cassava roots to be used as a base for the soup.

After greeting the chief, he had us sit down at a rustic table and proceeded to serve us lunch. The missionaries had brought sandwiches with them for me for they knew I would not eat from the village pot. They confided that, "We have missionaries that have been here over twenty years, and they would never dare to eat that food! Our stomachs are just not up to it!"

I refused the sandwiches, and the old chief, with a big smile on his face, served me a large bowl of soup. First, he placed a good helping of cassava in the granite bowl and then covered that with the mixture from the pot. You would never ask, or even think about, the contents. One ingredient was very hot peppers in abundance.

But, I was hungry and surprisingly, it was very good! I had seconds! I did, silently, pray a very sincere prayer for God's blessing on the food.

After, lunch, we all gathered under a large arbor they had built for this occasion, and I was privileged to preach the Gospel to this tribe who was hearing it for the second time. After returning home, I sent the missionaries funds to build them a church.

After the many wonderful experiences in Africa, we boarded a plane out of Accra and flew to Athens, Greece. We had contributed toward the new church and were there to preach a ten night dedication revival.

A beautiful high rise building had just been completed in the very heart of Athens. We bought two floors of the building for our church there. One floor was the auditorium and the other one was for the Sunday school and offices. It was a real time of blessing as we ministered to those people.

I made it a point to preach on Mars Hill where the Apostle Paul preached so long ago. We stayed in a hotel there but were entertained for a late dinner every night by Jerry and Mary Metaxatou in their home.

He was a high-ranking officer in the Greek army and was over the entire medical division. He was a member of our church. They lived on a hillside overlooking the Parthenon and the Acropolis. We were in awe at the "Light and Sound" exhibition every night. We really had ring-side seats!

The colonel had, without our knowledge, arranged a departure for us that we will never forget. The plane was ready for take off. We had said our goodbyes. He stepped out in front of the large group waiting to board, raised his hand and, as he was in dress uniform, got everyone's attention. In a commanding voice he said loudly, "Everyone stay right where you are. The Dodds will board first." Then a couple of soldiers unrolled a red carpet out to the plane, and we were escorted to it.

As we proceeded, Francine said aside to me, "Can you believe this?"

I replied, "Don't hesitate, just keep on walking!" We three boarded first! We were God's ambassadors!

On the flight back to Rome, we were really looked over by our fellow passengers as they tried to discover who these "important" people were.

From Rome, we flew over the Alps, around the Matterhorn and landed in Zurich, Switzerland. We enjoyed, so much, a few days of rest and relaxation after we were finally in a hotel room. There was a big convention there and no rooms were available. As a last resort, I contacted the hotel I had stayed in alone a few years before. They had one room available, and, to our delight, it was the same room I had previously stayed in. Switzerland did not disappoint us. The food was good; we especially enjoyed the rosebud jellies served at breakfast.

We had perfect flights on to Paris, then to London, to Iceland, New York, and finally to Tulsa. Home! What a sweet word.

While pastoring at Broken Arrow, I visited a lot in nursing homes and was astonished to see our people in the sub-standard housing. It was a discouraging thing. I determined to do something about it. I bought acreage on South Main. I had a friend in the higher echelon of the F.H.A. tell me that he would get a loan for me that would cover the building and all the contents, furniture and all. He wanted a nice place for his aunt to live. So, we built a sixty-two bed first class nursing home, hired RNs and staff and filled it up really soon. How we enjoyed ministering to the dear people who were no longer able to care for themselves. And, during this time, I was appointed by the Governor to a committee to set the standards for all Oklahoma nursing homes. But, after operating this facility for almost five years, I found the pressure of my church work, including my state and national positions was pretty demanding. I sold the home, and it is still one of the premier nursing homes in this area. Francine and I continued to pastor the Broken Arrow Assembly, and it continued to grow.

Toward the end of our pastorate, our daughter Jimmie introduced us to a unique business opportunity. The Amway experience. I saw the big picture at once. My view went beyond the moving of products to the realm of reaching people and giving them a helping hand up. Because of our success, I became friends with the winners, the diamonds, double diamonds, etc. In fact, we arrived at the diamond level ourselves and had two diamonds in our line, one of which was my brother, Doyce, and his wife.

My vision was soon realized. Francine and I were special speakers for some of the largest conventions throughout the nation. We spoke at the Dallas meeting, the New Orleans one, etc. One of our biggest and most successful ones was the convention in Philadelphia. That great crowd embraced our success, and I can still hear the group of about 10,000 singing, "We love those Dodds ... we love those Dodds!"

Francine and I both told our story and taught them the elements of success on Fridays and Saturdays. Then, on Sunday mornings I was free to preach to those great crowds as I pleased. It was indeed a religious service with many hundreds of decisions for Christ! Francine was at her best in these meetings. She really shined, and the people loved her. Our involvement with this organization gave us much satisfaction, and we have many memories of the hundreds of friends we have made.

A glimpse of the spunk of my feisty sweetheart ...

We took a large group to Colorado to ski. We took one lesson on the kid's slope, and Francine took the lift to the top of the mountain. I thought she was just going along with the experienced people to enjoy the view. But, I looked through my binoculars and saw her take off to ski down the mountain. She made it a short way and fell. The next thing I knew, she had her skis off and was walking down the middle of the ski slope, with experienced skiers going around her on both sides. I couldn't stand the suspense so I sent the rescue crew up after her. She argued with them but finally got in their sled and was brought down. The first words out of her mouth were, "Why did you send them after me? I was having a great time!" Life was never dull.

My brother, Doyce, and his wife, Nadine, shared many wonderful experiences with us. One unforgettable time was when we rented a car in Hawaii and toured the north shore as well as the main downtown areas. We ate at out of the way places, explored to our heart's content, let the women have time to shop; what a happy time!

After pastoring Broken Arrow Assembly for thirty-six years, we felt it was time to give someone else that responsibility. Our good friends, Tom and Darlene Goins, came and did a great job of pastoring this church for seventeen years. Those were years of growth and blessing.

Doyce's wife was such a help to Francine as her health began to break. She regularly came by to take her to appointments for nail care. It was a special time of shared friendship. And, she also spent many hours in the hospitals with her, remembering with her the good times.

Much to my sorrow, I saw my beautiful, vivacious wife beginning to decline in health. Our house became a burden to her, and I began thinking of finding some place that would give us all the facilities we really needed and be more compact in space.

My sister, Berline, and husband, Bob, recently purchased a home that met all our specifications in a new gated community. We visited with them, and Francine exclaimed, "Honey, this is what I want. I want it just like this one." So, I bought the one that had just been started across the road and had it finished out as quickly as possible.

Meanwhile, I placed our home on the market, and it sold in six days! A miracle of God's provision. But, while in that home for more than a year I took care of my sweetheart, night and day, by myself. I was glad to be able to do it. Both of my girls would come when they could, but their commitments kept them away.

It was a happy day when our new home was finished, and we were able to move in. Somehow, I felt that this would boost my wife's awareness, and she did show some excitement as she watched the girls place her furniture in the rooms.

I did everything I could think of to further her interest in her new home. The dining area has sliding glass doors overlooking the back yard area. Barbara and I bought a bird feeder and hung it on the fence. I would bring her in every morning and position her where she could look at her birds. She had "Big Red," a beautiful red bird, and his mate, a great company of doves, and a vast assortment of other kinds of sweet singing birds. As she ate her meager breakfast, I would talk to her about her favorite ones.

She only enjoyed her home for a few weeks as her health was going fast. I would get her up at night. As she was completely helpless, I could not get her back in bed and would have to call Jimmie to help me.

Jimmie saw the heavy load I was carrying, so she quit her job and came to our home to assist me. I could not have continued much longer were it not for my sweet girls.

The hospital stays began. First, the Broken Arrow Hospital, then Saint Francis, and finally the specialty hospital in Tulsa. We never left her alone, day or night. One or both of us was always at her side. During these stressful times, Barbara would come and stay for weeks, as long as she possibly could without losing her job. She insisted on taking nights, and she shared wonderful memories with Mom during those night hours.

When the physicians said they had done all they could for Mom in a hospital setting, we knew we had to move her to a skilled nursing facility. She chose for us by saying, "I want to go to the same place where Berline is!"

Meanwhile, Jimmie's constant care for Francine both in the hospitals and nursing home, made her to be completely dependent on her. She deferred every decision saying, "Ask Jimmie." They would hold hands at night and talk the hours away. Each morning, I would greet her, "There's my sweetheart!" She looked forward to an old-fashioned donut and coffee.

Through it all, she remained the same wonderful, sweet Francine. She knew she was not going to get well and told me so. While my heart was breaking, we had many confidential and private moments as I attempted to answer her questions. During these last days, we passed our seventieth wedding anniversary and her eighty-eighth birthday. She scarcely took note of either. She was living more on the other side than she was here. She talked with her mother and daddy and Lum. She asked us if we saw them … she was almost home before her actual departure. She called me to her side and asked that I tell her about heaven. With my heart so full I could hardly speak, I told her of the beauties of that place that was illumined by the light of the Savior's face, of the reunions. When I told her of our families being together again, she whispered, "Oh, that's what I want!"

We shared many precious moments … memories that will live in my heart forever.

I was leafing through Francine's Bible recently and ran across this notation, written in her hand: "Death cannot separate you if you refuse to let it!"

I refuse to let it! She told me one night, "Don't forget me!" How could I? She has been a big part of my life for over seventy years. She is still my wife. She is in my dreams almost every night. I reach over in bed to make sure she is okay. I listen for the sound of her voice. I yearn for the touch of her hand. I so want to talk over the day's events with her. Those wonderful blessings will have to wait for a little while.

Another note, written by her hand, I found in her Bible:

People who love dearly never grow old …

they may die of old age but they die young.

Don't resent growing old,

it's a privilege denied to many!

One night we discussed who would go first. I told her that I thought I would. She emphatically said, "No, I know I'll be going first!" And then we made a pact. We agreed that whoever went first would linger near the Eastern gate, and we would meet just inside the gate … to be together forever!

Just a few nights before she went home, she called Jimmie to come close to her so she could hear her. I had just gone home to get a little rest. She took Jimmie's hand and said, "Honey, I may not be here in the morning. If I'm not, tell Daddy I'll meet him just inside the gate!"

I had shared with her a vision God had previously given me of heaven. Just a glimpse, but what a revelation! I found myself walking toward the celestial city. I walked slowly up a beautiful pathway toward the entrance. The River of Life flowed so gently along on my right, and I reveled in the beauty of the fruit trees with their abundance of fruits of all kinds.

I came to the very gate and looked inside. What indescribable beauty! The whole city glowed with the light of His presence.

Then I saw my family... everyone who had gone before, rushing toward me. They were so happy, laughing and shouting, "Here comes James!" Mother, Father, Sister, Brother, a real crowd.

And right behind them a great multitude of people, and I recognized that here were the ones that Francine and I had spent our lifetime winning for Jesus! They were shouting, "Here comes our old pastor!"

The vision faded. I could not go inside. It wasn't my time. I needed to stay awhile, to watch over my girls... to point my grandchildren and great-grandchildren to the only true light. For I want all of us to be there together.

I will always appreciate the times Pastor Goldsmith came to Francine's room to talk to her and pray. He was there when my sweetheart drew her last breath and went peacefully into the presence of the Lord she adored. He and his wife, Debbie, have shown us kindness and respect.

Also, Pastor and Mrs. James Holder, Rev. and Mrs. Tom Goins, Dr. and Mrs. Armon Newburn, and Rev. and Mrs. H.A. Burmmett, all good personal friends, came by for prayer and encouragement. Others prayed.

So, I am here, living alone in the little home I bought for Francine. I suppose I'll be here until I go on or until Jesus comes again.

I expect to move to that city quite soon. I can almost see my feisty little sweetheart saying to one of her angels, "I've waited long enough... come go with me and we'll get James and bring him home!"

What a happy day! I have no fear of death for I know in Whom I have believed and am persuaded that He will have a place for me somewhere in that magnificent city. And, His plan will include my sweetheart of more than seventy years being by my side as we prepare to welcome our family home!

My journey will at last be complete!

Images throughout the Years

Dedication

No story of my journey could be complete without recognizing the great contribution of my sweet wife, Francine. She accompanied me on this amazing trip for seventy wonderful years. She shared my triumphs, my disappointments, my joys, my fears. Without her, I could never have lived the exciting life God gave me. She was involved in every decision we made as we journeyed together. Her counsel spared me many hurts and kept me in the center of God's will. So, I lovingly dedicate this book to her ... she is in heaven but she knows.

About the Author

Dr. James C. Dodd

The world has been his pulpit: Born March 11, 1918, in Fayetteville, Arkansas, to Rev. and Mrs. Berl M. Dodd. Married his childhood sweetheart, Francine Bush, on August 25, 1935. Francine went to heaven on November 5, 2005.

Dr. Dodd has two daughters, four grandchildren and four great-grandchildren, and he now resides in his home in Tulsa, Oklahoma.

James C. Dodd was born on March 11, 1918, in Fayetteville, Arkasas. The son of Rev. and Mrs. Berl Dodd, James was next to the eldest of four children.

Francine H. Bush was born in Seminole, Oklahoma. Being next to the youngest of seven children, three were boys and four were girls.

Our teenage courting days

I played first chair for the trombone section of the Seminole, Oklahoma High School Band

The

Mother, Dad, my sister Berniece, and myself.

My dad and sweet mother.

Grandma and Grandpa Bogan, grandparents on mother's side

This house was the home of my Grandpa Bob Dodd and family

Beginnings

The four Dodd siblings.

Dad brings one in the
Pacific Ocean. He always
wore his suit when fishing!

Francine

Me, Doyce and Berline

The

Francine with Ileene, Delmer and June

Mom and Dad Bush

The whole family of siblings

Beginnings

Original church building when we arrived in 1942.

My boys, the original "Commandos for Christ". They are now successful businessmen and they occupy many places of ministry in their church.

The Church at

Radio choir, during our rebuilding of the church building, faithfully continue to sing from temporary quarters in the youth building.

Broken Arrow Assemblies of God Youth Camp at one of the state campgrounds. Wonderful days of fun and worship.

Broken Arrow

The pastor, at home with his family.

The "Country Parson" (me) leading the Broken Arrow Rooster Day Parade, an annual event that drew thousands of spectators every year.

The devil was a part of the parade one year and drew a lot of response. In fact, he had to be rescued and brought back to the church. I put him there to draw attention, and it sure did!

The Church at

Pastor and family stand proudly before the new church.

The tragic scene as it goes up completely in flames. This photo appeared on the cover of Christian Life magazine.

Broken Arrow

Copy of a letter I received from Clyde W. Wright, Mayor of Broken Arrow upon my resigning as pastor of the Broken Arrow Assembly.

Office of
MAYOR

P R O C L A M A T I O N

WHEREAS, James C. Dodd has been Pastor of the Broken Arrow Assembly of God Church for thirty-six years and has led it from 125 members to nearly 1,000 members; and

WHEREAS, Pastor Dodd has gained a reputation as one of the most eloquent ministers in and around Broken Arrow; and

WHEREAS, Pastor Dodd had become the youngest minister elected as Sectional Presbyter, served as Assistant Superintendent of the Oklahoma District Council, served as a member of the Board of Regents of the General Presbytery Board of Regents, and has been named to "Who's Who in Oklahoma"; and

WHEREAS, Pastor Dodd and his wife Francine, whom he calls "a very vital part to my ministry", will now take their ministries overseas to Europe, the Middle East and South America.

NOW, THEREFORE, I, CLYDE W. WRIGHT, Mayor of the City of Broken Arrow, Oklahoma, in recognition of Pastor Dodd's many accomplishments, do hereby proclaim Saturday and Sunday, July 15th and 16th, as "James C. Dodd Appreciation Days" in the City of Broken Arrow.

IN WITNESS WHEREOF, I have hereunto set my hand and caused the Seal of the City of Broken Arrow to be affixed on this twelfth day of July in the year of Our Lord one thousand nine hundred seventy-eight.

_____
Mayor

ATTEST:

_____
City Clerk

City of Broken Arrow
P.O. Box 610, Broken Arrow, Oklahoma 74012   918—251—5311

Copy of a letter I received from my good friend, Dr. Thomas F. Zimmerman, General Superintendent of the Assemblies of God, upon my resigning the Broken Arrow Church

THE GENERAL COUNCIL OF THE ASSEMBLIES OF GOD

1445 BOONVILLE AVENUE

SPRINGFIELD, MISSOURI 65802

THOS. F. ZIMMERMAN
GENERAL SUPERINTENDENT

May 31, 1978

TELEPHONE
(417) 862-2781

The Rev. James C. Dodd, Pastor
Assembly of God
305 North Main
Broken Arrow, Oklahoma 74012

Dear Brother Dodd:

On behalf of the General Council of the Assemblies of God, I wish to commend you for your 36 years of fruitful ministry during which time you have served as the distinguished pastor of the Assemblies of God church in Broken Arrow. We deeply appreciate your exemplary life, as well as your efficient leadership. You have built faithfully and well. Eternity will be made richer as a result of your God-anointed ministry.

May God give you a wonderful sense of fulfillment as you look upon the many sheaves which you will be able to lay at the Master's feet.

I personally esteem you highly and want you to know of our love and prayers for your future ministry.

Sincerely yours,

Thos. F. Zimmerman
General Superintendent

What a joy it was to preach in the church at Andria, that our church built for the impoverished people. Francine loved the Africans and mixed with them and was accepted by all.

Broken Arrow Assembly gave the money to purchase the two floors of this large building which houses the Evangelistic Center in Athens, Greece.

A picture of the crowd attending one of the services of the 10 day dedication revival which Pastor Dodd conducted.

A Few of

Barbara is seen here with the little chimps who lived on the compound. She spent hours sitting on the grass, telling Bible stories to the leper children.

The school children taught by two of our lady missionaries.
"Ma" Steidel, as she was called by her beloved lepers, spent her life ministering to them. She built this village, and any leper could come and live with his family and be treated. We spent over a week ministering twice daily and seeing many brought to Christ.

Our Missions

I preached in this church that is carved out of solid rock.
Every home in this unique city is a cave.

Part of the crowd at Messina that
could not squeeze in.

A Few of

I'm standing at the mid-point of "No Man's Land." I had been escorted through the Mandelbaum Gate, early one Sunday morning, to this point by the Arabian authorities. I waited at this battle scarred building until the Jewish delegation arrived to escort me the rest of the way into Jewish Jerusalem.

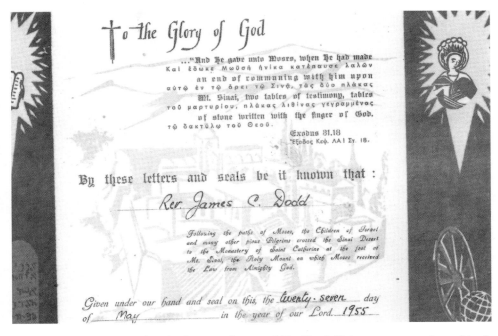

Certificate awarded me for climbing to the top of Mt. Sinai. This was an experience I had before the mountain was closed off to everyone.

Our Missions

I Walked in Petra

Israel's City of Refuge

Some of the greatest thrills of my life have come to me in the land of Israel. How awesome to walk in the midst of fulfilled prophecy! I saw what Isaiah wrote about when he said, "And He shall set up an ensign for the nations, and shall assemble the outcasts of Israel, and gather together the dispersed of Judah from the four corners of the earth" (Isaiah 11:12).

Israel is a nation; her flag is flying, her hundreds of thousands have found a home. And these Jews have come from the remote places of the earth desiring to live in peace in the land God promised to them so long ago. But much suffering is ahead for these peculiar people who have been preserved by God to this day.

Early one morning in June, we boarded a Jordanian plane at the airport in Arab Jerusalem. We flew over the northern part of the Dead Sea, past the ancient city of Ma'an and on toward the waste howling wilderness. Upon landing at a military airport in the desert, we transferred to a car and drove for two hours. Then, at an outpost of the Arab Legion we left the cars and mounted horses for the last five miles of our journey.

Finally, we came to the rose-red city of Esau, situated deep in the desert of southern Jordan, 180 miles south of Amman, the capital. When I rode through the "Sig," the narrow rock defile leading to Petra, and suddenly came face to face with "Ed Deir" or the temple, I gasped in utter amazement. I saw the omnipotent wisdom of a loving Heavenly Father in that He has prepared for future occupancy a vast city of refuge. But before we describe this city further, let us look into the scripture and see a few of the events which will lead up to its use.

The next event on God's prophetic calendar is, without doubt, the catching away of the Bride of Christ, the prepared church. We believe this will occur before the great tribulation that is to come soon. Jesus said, "Watch ye therefore, and pray always, that ye may be accounted worthy to escape all these things that shall come to pass, and to stand before the Son of Man" (Luke 21:36). This is the hope of the church. We shall soon be caught up with Him to attend the marriage supper of the Lamb and appear at the judgment seat of Christ. These events will take approximately seven years as we count time here on earth.

But the scene on earth during that same week of years will be an entirely different picture. The antichrist is reigning; that great deceiver makes a covenant with the Jews and re-establishes the temple worship. He is antichrist all the time, but his beastly nature is not evident at first. But at the "middle of the week," after the war in the heavenlies between Michael and Satan, when Satan is cast out of that domain, there is a significant change. It is as if the mask is

Glorious Petra!
Berline and Francine at the
entrance of the treasury.

pulled off and this man, indwelt by the devil, reveals his true self.

In Revelation 12, which deals with this period, two wonders appear in heaven. In verse one we read of a "sun-clothed woman." What does she represent? The virgin Mary? The Church? Much study has led me to the conclusion that she represents neither Mary nor the Church, but Israel.

Israel is repeatedly described in scripture as a married woman. After her period of rejection she is described as a widow. Again, as a divorced wife. Again, as an adulterous wife. Now, as the "sun-clothed woman," she is described as being "with child" and in "travail to bring forth." (The Church is always pictured in the Word as a virgin, espoused to one husband, and nowhere is it even intimated that she will be a mother.)

In Romans 9:5, speaking of Israel,

Paul declares, "Of whom, as concerning the flesh, Christ came." Isaiah looked forward to the time when Israel could say, "Unto us a child is born; unto us a Son is given." Before Christ was born, Israel had to pass through sore afflictions and judgments, a time of travail. She accomplished her time. Now, in Revelation 12:5 we see the result of her travail: "And she brought forth a man child, who was to rule all nations with a rod of iron; and her child was caught up unto God, and to His throne." This man child, caught up to the throne, is now seated at the right hand of power in the heavenlies.

Verse six describes the flight of the woman into the wilderness to escape the wrath of the antichrist. Between these two verses lies the present church age—which John omits, since he is not dealing with the church.

"And when the dragon saw that he was cast unto the earth, he persecuted the woman which brought forth the man child. And to the woman were given two wings of a great eagle, that she might fly into the wilderness, into her place, where she is nourished for a time, and times, and half a time, from the face of the serpent" (Revelation 12:13,14). This explicitly declares the time to be three and one-half years, or the latter half of the great tribulation. This scripture takes us back to Israel's flight from Egypt. God said to them in Exodus 19:4, "Ye have seen what I did unto the Egyptians, and how I bare you to Myself." Just as the woman and the dragon are symbols, so the eagle's wings are symbols of a rapid flight into the wilderness where she is nourished of God for three and one-half years.

Isaiah says of this time, "Come, my people (Israel), enter into thy chambers, and shut thy doors about thee; hide thyself as it were for a little moment until the indignation be overpast." Jesus said, "When ye therefore shall see the abomination of desolation, spoken of by Daniel the prophet,

More Petra.
Tomb of Sextius Florentinus.
A great example of Hellenistic architecture.

stand in the holy place... then let them which be in Judaea flee into the mountains..." (Matthew 24:15).

Let us return now to the actual flight of the "woman" and locate the place to which she will go for safety. The cities of refuge God designated for the children of Israel in the early days of their history are good types of this city of refuge. These were places to which the manslayer could go for refuge from the avenger of blood. If it was proved that the hunted man was guilty of willful murder, he was turned over to the avenger. If not, he was protected, but he had to remain in the city until the death of the high priest. Now we find the Jews fleeing to a city of refuge.

The Jewish race caused the death of Christ. They cried, "His blood be upon us and upon our children!" At first this appears to be willful murder, but hear the prayer of Jesus: "Father, forgive them, for they know not what they do." Paul says, "Had they known it they would not have crucified the Lord of Glory." So this places them in the same classification as the manslayer fleeing from the avenger of blood. They have been running toward this city of refuge for over 1,900 years, hounded from nation to nation, fulfilling the prophecy of Moses that they would "find no rest for the soles of their feet."

Speaking of this time and of the antichrist, Daniel says, "He shall also enter into the glorious land, and many countries shall be overthrown; but these shall escape out of his hand; even Edom, and Moab, and the chief of the children of Ammon."

Isaiah said, "Let mine outcasts dwell with thee, Moab, be thou a covert to them from the face of the spoiler..." (Isaiah 16:4). In Edom, in this wilderness that God says shall not be touched by the forces of antichrist, is situated this city of refuge, Petra.

Called "Sela" in the Bible, the

city is also called "Seir," "Mount Seir," or the "Mountains of Esau." Genesis 36:8, 9 identifies Esau as father of the Edomites, the builders of this rocky city: "Thus dwelt Esau in Mount Sier: Esau is Edom. And these are the generations of Esau the father of the Edomites in Mount Seir."

Saul fought against this city,

The Khazneh, which has become the symbol of Petra.

David fought against it and prevailed; Joab conquered it.

Petra was a great commercial center in the time of Solomon. In A.D. 105, the Romans took it over and called it "Arabia Petra." It fell into the hands of the Arabs and became a lost civilization from the seventh century until 1812 when it was re-discovered. This vast, silent city has only one entrance—a narrow, winding defile, at places only twelve feet wide and then up to forty feet. The sides of this entrance are precipitous, 200 to 1,000 feet high, and lined with monuments and carvings from bygone centuries.

Once inside this rocky enclosure, the traveler stands spellbound as he views the ruins of magnificent buildings carved into the solid rock. The colorful cliffs are honeycombed with excavations up to 300 feet high.

I believe, from a comparison of scripture, that this rocky fastness, this ancient city, could very well be Israel's city of refuge. When the accumulated dust of centuries is swept away, an entire city will welcome the thousands of weary Jews who will seek respite from war.

We read that then the antichrist will cast a flood of water out of his mouth to try to destroy his escaping prey. But the earth will open its mouth and swallow the flood. Antichrist will send his armies after the fleeing Israelites, but these armies will be swallowed by the desert (possibly by a great sand storm).

Israel will be safe in her place of refuge until the return of the great High Priest, Who shall come with the armies of heaven to effect her complete deliverance. Then, and only then, will she be enabled to leave her place of refuge.

I walked in this place. I visualized the caves peopled with countless thousands of Jews, sustained as Israel was during the forty years of wilderness journeying. I walked among scenes of future prophetic significance. The glow will remain in my heart till He comes.

The battle scarred entrance into one of the gates.

The Eastern gate, which will remain closed until Jesus returns

A Few of

Two of the gates into the city

Our Missions

Our 50TH anniversary, sponsored by our two girls, Jimmie and Barbara. We couldn't realize that we would have twenty more years together!
Francine and I cut the cake after we renewed our vows.

Our two beautiful daughters, Barbara and Jimmie with us.

At Home

Top left photo shows Pastor and Francine at one of the great conventions where they both spoke and ministered. Two photos with Doyce and Nadine, then enjoying a Hawaiian feast. The plane is the one we flew to many of our conventions.

and Beyond

Lum and I with the 11 pound catfish I caught from his pond.

At Home

Fishing!
Fishing trips I took with Dr. Goggin and Russell Herndon to Padre Island
when the King Fish were running.

and Beyond

Bill and Kimberlee Nash

Dave and Candice Reid

Keith and Jackie Belknap

Joe and Lindsay Manscuso

Inside

Little Billy as he recovers from leukemia.

Now, Billy as a strong young man speaking at the annual New Year's Eve fundraiser for the Kid's Camp for traumatized kids in Houston. This camp is sponsored by our granddaughter, Kim, and her husband, Bill absolutely no charge to any of the children. A place to repair and heal broken hearts, minds and bodies

Our Family

Letter from Candice

The first thing I remember after the fall was waking up on the stretcher in the emergency department. Every part of me was in unimaginable pain. I begged to see Dave, but the doctors and nurses were working too frantically to even respond to my request. They wheeled me by Dave on the way to another part of the hospital. I heard him say that he called my parents and my mom was on her way. She would catch the first flight from Connecticut to Illinois in the morning. But they wouldn't stop to even let me hold his hand even for a second.

I really don't know how to describe the fear and pain. I asked anyone who walked by, "Will I be able to walk again? Will I be able to run?" No one would answer me. I have never felt more alone. That's when I started to pray. I remember just saying, "God, please help me" over and over again.

And then from nowhere, my cousin Keith was standing at the foot of the bed. It took me a second to recognize him because I could barely make out his face. My eyes were swollen from crying so many silent tears. I hadn't seen him in several years even though we lived in the same town. I think he smiled at me. He may have said something, but I honestly don't remember. I just remember his smile. It gave me enormous peace and strength.

Once I saw him, I knew it was going to all be okay. I didn't know how, but his presence gave me the strength I so desperately needed. I absolutely do not know how I would have made it through the night without him.

There are so many people that helped me heal emotionally and physically from my injuries. Dave, my mom, my sister, and my grandparents in particular played critical roles. But Keith was the first person to help me on that journey and for that I will be forever grateful.

I will never be able to say thank you in a way that can fully express what he did for me that night. I will always feel a special connection to him and I would do anything for Keith and his family.

I actually wouldn't change anything that happened that night. It taught me the power of prayer and family that has in some way impacted every day of my life since.

—Candice

This is our miracle granddaughter and her letter to our grandson Keith, who was the first of the family to arrive at the Chicago trauma center where the doctors were battling to save her life. Thank God, miracles happen today!

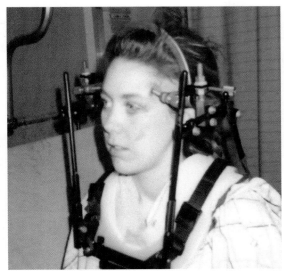

Jimmie's family, New Years Eve 2007

James C. Nash

Jimmie
and
Barbara

Christina J. Belknap

William D. Nash, Jr.

Keith L. Belknap III

Barbara's Family, Christmas
2006

Inside

Order from
EVANGELIST AND MRS. JAMES C. DODD
Box 1428, Seminole, Oklahoma

As young evangelists we were requested to sing "When I've Gone the Last Mile of the Way" scores of times as the pastor, and the family loved it too. So, at our last Christmas together, they requested we sing it for them one more time. We did our best. Although Francine struggled, she bravely sung it with me.

Our Family

THE WHITE HOUSE
WASHINGTON

We are saddened to know of your loss. May you be surrounded and strengthened by the love of family and friends during this difficult time. Our thoughts and prayers are with you.

Sincerely,

George Bush   *Laura Bush*

We received so many cards, letters, phone calls, internet messages that it would be impossible to show them all here. So, we decided to show the one message from President and Mrs. Bush and let it represent all our precious friends.

Facing page: Sunrise over Jerusalem! Mal. 4:2 "But for you who fear My name, the sun of righteousness will arise with healing in His wings!"

TOO MUCH TO GAIN TO LOSE
words by Dottie Rambo

Too many miles behind me,
Too many trials are through;
Too many tears help me to remember,
There's too much to gain to lose.

Too many sunsets lie behind the mountains,
Too many rivers my feet have walked through;
Too many treasures are waiting over yonder,
There's too much to gain to lose.